THE FOUR
ESSENTIALS
OF
CHRISTIANITY

JIM PIPER

THE FOUR ESSENTIALS OF CHRISTIANITY
© 2008 by Jim Piper

ISBN: 0-9793192-3-4
978-0-9793192-3-5

Published by

LIFEBRIDGE
BOOKS
P.O. BOX 49428
CHARLOTTE, NC 28277

Printed in the United States of America.

CONTENTS

INTRODUCTION

In every discipline of life, essentials are the fundamentals. They are the foundation on which everything else is built. Regardless of the subject, when the approach is wrong the result is in danger. The same is true in the precious revelation of Christianity. The essentials must be known and practiced so that the faith which is expressed comes from a solid basis.

There are four basics to Christianity: one truth in Christ with four recurring commitments. Believers must practice these imperatives over and over again. The four essentials are: Knowing Christ, Following Christ, Becoming like Christ, Reproducing Christ in others.

Knowing the Savior will you help you develop a deeper trust for God, following Him will require devotion, becoming like Christ in character will be the supernatural result of knowing and devoting yourself to Him, and reproducing Jesus in others will be a mission you joyfully embrace.

I have written this book with two types of people in mind. The first is the believer who has faithfully attended and supported the local church, but knows something is missing in his or her spiritual foundation. The second is the new believer looking for clear and practical direction.

The vision of this work is to lay a solid yet simple spiritual base straight from the pages of Holy Scripture. I also include as an introduction to each lesson, stories and thoughts from my personal experiences as a follower of Jesus Christ, a father, husband, pastor and church planter. My prayer for this book is that it will serve as a guide for personal devotion to Jesus, providing spiritual nourishment to you and to the church.

– Jim Piper

KNOWING CHRIST

On every journey there must be a starting point, and the first essential of life and Christianity is to know God through Jesus Christ. Increasing your knowledge of Him will increase your trust in God and transform your world view.

From a horizontal perspective, you have learned that some people can be trusted and some cannot. The individuals you have confidence in are probably those who have done you little or no harm over the years. They have proven their faithfulness to you and to those you love. Together, your relationship has been tested and it has matured. You can speak truthfully to one another without fear of creating an incurable fracture, and you could and would call on them at any time if the need arose. For that matter, you would run to help them if they needed you. These ideas paint a picture of the ideal behind friendships and healthy relationships.

When it comes to our relationships, is there anything more important than trust? It is the *blood* of friendship. The problem for most of us is that we do not give enough time and effort to our relationships in order to build and experience a fellowship of such ideals. This is especially true of our partnership with God.

Life can be confusing and difficult. Knowing we have a home in heaven because of the faith God has given us in the person and work of Jesus Christ certainly can ease the blow of life's circumstances. However, without improving our knowledge of God through Christ, we will remain ignorant, uniformed and often become unable to cope with or accept the difficulties of life. When this happens, we begin to lose trust in God. This is a tragedy because if there is anyone who is consistent and unchanging, it is the living Christ—God the Son.

We will never understand why the Lord desires our full devotion until we know Him as He longs to be known. We will never trust until we know He can be trusted. Many of us are ready to die because of the grace of heaven, yet few of us are ready to live because we know Him only from a distance. He may live in you, but He desperately desires to live *with* you and *through* you.

~1~
The Invisible

*All honor and glory to God forever and
ever! He is the eternal King, the unseen one
who never dies; he alone is God.*
− 1 Timothy 1:17

Rarely have I doubted the existence of a Supreme Being. To me, the reality of God is not a difficult concept to believe. When I am at rest and listen to the pounding of ocean waves or ponder the majestic Rocky Mountain Range, God's presence is absorbed into my empty places. When I become more inquisitive and consider the consciousness and power of humanity to choose and create, God's fingerprint rises to the surface of my mind. Then, when I hear of great evils done to the innocent, screams from within demand justice, awakening the divine morality hidden deep in the forgotten places of my heart.

Pondering the hand of God on creation and morality helps me see the outline of the invisible God. The totality of Scripture teaches us that the Almighty is both invisible and visible to the human senses. He is invisible in that He is Spirit and transcends the best of human understanding and vocabulary. He is visible in the sense of revelation—how He has revealed Himself to humankind, His own creation.

Many are trying to figure out how God can become relevant to their lives, when instead they should be wondering if they are relevant to God. The Father defines us; we do not define Him. After all, it is simple logic to recognize that the created exists for the purposes of the Creator, not the other way around.

The fundamental pursuit of theology—the study of God—is

based upon what the Almighty revealed about Himself to us. We conclude that whatever God has uncovered must be important because it tells us not only who He is, but also the reasons for our existence. The quest for understanding what God has revealed is what makes the invisible God visible to our minds and our senses.

HOW HAS GOD REVEALED HIMSELF?

God has revealed Himself in creation.

Romans 1:18-20 explains it this way: *"But God shows his anger from heaven against all sinful, wicked people who suppress the truth by their wickedness. They know the truth about God because he has made it obvious to them. For ever since the world was created, people have seen the earth and sky. Through everything God made, they can clearly see his invisible qualities—his eternal power and divine nature. So they have no excuse for not knowing God."*

In many ways we toil with the realm of creation. We climb mountains, cross bodies of waters, plow the hard ground and take shelter from excessive elements which come with the cold of winter and the heat of summer. But even in our toil, we marvel at creation. We ponder its beauty and majesty—and are amazed at the divine statements of mountain peaks, crashing waves on the shore, prairies filled with natural flowers, wooded lakes and starry skies.

We are also amazed by animal life. We stop our cars to stare at a deer in the woods. Some invest a great amount of time and money to venture into the wilderness to hunt, study and photograph the amazing scenes of God's creatures in the far corners of the planet. We are curious, and somehow feel that part of our identity can be found in the wilderness.

The advancement of humanity also tells a story of God, and our questions and discoveries are ongoing. Our ability to solve many human problems has evolved into what we call disciplines of study. We now know the lessons of human behavior as psychology, study of the stars as astronomy and have the disciplines of art, engineering, mathematics, aerospace, business, education, biology, philosophy, technology, linguistics, medicine, and the list goes on. We are no longer satisfied with learning about the earth; we desire to know more about what is hidden in the galaxies.

By learning through these fields of study, we see the different ways He has revealed himself through creation and begin to see more of God. In a holistic sense, *all* the human disciplines pursue the knowledge of the Almighty. Even though every student would not confess such a thing, it does not make it any less true. Human behavior reveals the truth written in the verses above. God is revealing Himself to His creation *within* creation.

God has revealed Himself in Jesus Christ.

The word Gospel means "Good News"—and the Father made Himself known through His Son, who is God in the flesh.

This is explained in the first few verses in the New Testament book of Hebrews: *"Long ago God spoke many times and in many ways to our ancestors through the prophets. And now in these final days, he has spoken to us through his Son. God promised everything to the Son as an inheritance, and through the Son he created the universe. The Son radiates God's own glory and expresses the very character of God, and he sustains everything by the mighty power of his command. When he had cleansed us from our sins, he sat down in the place of honor at the right hand of the majestic God in heaven"* (Hebrews 1:1-3).

There are four life-changing truths in these verses which describe God's relationship to His Son, and Jesus' relationship to us.

First, the Almighty has a long track record for revealing Himself to human life. One such example is through the ancient prophets, and many of their words and actions are recorded in your Bible.

Second, the Father has revealed himself most clearly through Jesus Christ—the exact representation of God in character, mission and power!

Third, the Jesus we are learning to love, trust and serve is the very One holding all of creation together.

Fourth, Jesus is the gate keeper into the mercy and forgiveness of God. In short, anything we need to know about God we will see in Jesus.

God continues to reveal Himself as you worship Him.

So far we have discussed that the invisible God of the universe becomes visible as we follow the clues found in creation and we embrace the wonders of the Almighty in Jesus Christ. Appreciating creation is a good step in the process of knowing God—and believing in the person and life of Jesus Christ is critical. Yet, the knowledge of God does not become life-changing until you become an authentic worshiper. Since God is personally known through a dynamic relationship with the living Christ, only a supernaturally transformed soul can experience this fellowship. As we spend time in His presence, God is further revealed.

God must become your ultimate reality.

Your reality is not the experiences of your past, present or future—and is not your hopes, dreams, worries or fears. Your reality is *God*, because He transcends all we can experience on earth.

Whether you know it or not, you are in desperate need of Him since your eternity is in His hands. Your soul hungers to know God and to participate in a dynamic life-shaping fellowship with Him. Jesus explains in one simple sentence how this is accomplished: *"For God is Spirit, so those who worship him must worship in spirit and in truth"* (John 4:24).

PUTTING IT INTO PRACTICE

Learn to see the invisible God involved in the visible world. See His shadow in the wonders of creation and study the character and mission of God through Jesus Christ. Worship Him in Spirit and truth. Do not be satisfied with information received from others. Check it out yourself. Meditate on Romans 1:18-20 and Hebrews 1:1-3. Memorize and strive to understand the meaning of John 4:24.

POINTS TO PONDER

- What are some ways in which God has revealed Himself to mankind?
- What do you think it means to an "authentic worshiper"? How do we get to this point?
- How have you seen or witnessed the fingerprint of God?
- How does worshiping God help you to understand Him?
- In Hebrews 1:1-3 Scripture tells us God spoke to us through prophets, then through His Son Jesus Christ. How does God speak to you now?

~ 2 ~
CHRIST UP CLOSE

Then Jesus uttered another loud cry and breathed
his last. And the curtain in the sanctuary of the Temple
was torn in two, from top to bottom. When the Roman officer
who stood facing him saw how he had died, he exclaimed,
"Truly, this was the Son of God!"
— MARK 15:37-39

Have you ever been nose-to-nose with extreme poverty? Have you ever held a dying person in your hands? Have you ever experienced hell-like hate directed at you coming from another human being? Have you ever lost everything that ever mattered to you? If you answered "yes" to any of these questions, then you know the power of reality. Real stuff transforms our fantasy into humility.

Here's the crazy thing. Even though you experienced it first hand, words seem powerless to accurately communicate what you've endured. And this is exactly what happened to a Roman soldier who was nose-to-nose with the crucifixion of Jesus Christ. This soldier witnessed from a distance of yards, feet, and even inches the undiluted hatred people had for Jesus. The centurion saw the tears and the fears of those who loved Christ. He saw the blood splatter and the agony of crucifixion and rejection closer than a front row seat.

This soldier also saw divine love. He watched as Jesus reached out to one of the thieves being crucified next to Him. He saw a stubborn love that could only come from the strength of one who knows of a higher goal and a clear destination. This unnamed soldier met God in the flesh. The best words he could offer at that time were: *"Truly, this was the Son of God!"* (Mark 15:39).

WHO IS JESUS CHRIST UP CLOSE?

Christ is God the Son.

Though Jesus is known by many names, we must start with His most proper identity—He is God. To know Jesus as God introduces us to dimensions beyond our realm of understanding and leads us into a most mysterious fellowship and unity with the Almighty. To know Him is to have the opportunity of fellowship with God the Son, God the Father, and God the Holy Spirit. This spiritual dimension suggests there is one God in three distinct persons. Christianity calls this the Trinity or the Triune God. The names we have for God—Father, Son and Spirit—have been revealed to us by God.

The Father is God but He is not the Spirit or the Son; the Holy Spirit is God but not the Father or the Son; the Son is God but not the Father or the Spirit.

Since God is eternal, we know that Jesus has always existed. He was present before the incarnation—conceived by the Spirit and born of the virgin, Mary. His birth on earth was not His introduction to life; it was His action purposed to *give* life.

At the age of 30, Jesus being sinless, born without sin and remaining that way, began His three year ministry which would end with His death by crucifixion, resurrection, commission, and finally His ascension back to the realm of the divine community.

During His ministry on earth, Jesus' claim of divinity was well understood. During one of His conversations, some unbelieving Jews picked up rocks to stone Him because His claim to be God was so clear they viewed it to be profane and worthy of a death sentence which eventually was carried out by crucifixion.

We find this account in Scripture: *"'The Father and I are one.' Once again the people picked up stones to kill him. Jesus said, 'At my Father's direction I have done many good works. For which one are you going to stone me?' They replied, 'We're stoning you not for any good work, but for blasphemy! You, a mere man,*

15

claim to be God.'" (John 10:30-33).

In order for Jesus to accomplish His work on earth, His identity needed to be established. Though it would cause His death, this too was part of God's plan of redemption.

Christ was involved in creation.

By God's will and power He gave us the gift of life, and an environment which could sustain us. He made us as a reflection of Himself. The image of God in us is not physical but spiritual, emotional, relational, and includes the ability to choose and create.

The book of Genesis lets us in on God's conversation: *"Then God said, 'Let us make human beings in our image, to be like us. They will reign over the fish in the sea, the birds in the sky, the livestock, all the wild animals on the earth, and the small animals that scurry along the ground.' So God created human beings in his own image...male and female he created them. Then God blessed them and said, 'Be fruitful and multiply. Fill the earth and govern it. Reign over the fish in the sea, the birds in the sky, and all the animals that scurry along the ground'"* (Genesis 1:25-28).

Our Creator is indeed a giver who has bestowed on us amazing abilities and responsibilities.

To be more concise about Jesus, the New Testament clearly teaches that nothing exists which has not been created by the will and power of Christ. Many have come to believe that Jesus was a very good Man and a wonderful teacher of morals and human equality. Some even believe Jesus was so good that God decided to make Him a god. Because of these incomplete or incorrect ideas, the ones who actually walked with Jesus became more exact in their teaching. The apostle John makes it clear that Jesus is the creator of all things and all things have been made for His glory. John explains it this way: *"In the beginning the Word already existed. The Word was with God, and the Word was God. He existed in the beginning with God. God created everything through him, and nothing was created except through him....So the Word became human and made his home earth among us. He was full of unfailing love and faithfulness. And we have seen his glory, the glory of the Father's one and only Son"* (John 1:1-3,14).

The "Word" in the original language is "logos" and expresses many ideas of divinity. Some of these thoughts include the power of God, the thoughts of God, the will of God, and the words of God. With this understanding, we not only embrace another name for Jesus but can say in plain English that Jesus has always existed, He created everything, and He became flesh, revealing the unfailing love and faithfulness of God. To say Jesus is the only Son of the Father is to say that Jesus is the only One given by the Triune God to be God in the flesh for us all to see.

Christ is the Redeemer and Judge of all creation.

To "redeem" is to give one thing in exchange for something else. The birth, life, death, and resurrection of the Messiah—Jesus Christ—are given to liberate people from eternal death. Since God agreed to offer Jesus as Redeemer, He also agreed to make Him Judge over all creation. This makes sense because the only way a person can miss out on the mercy and grace of God's redemptive purposes is to reject the Redeemer Himself. Every person will stand before Christ and Jesus will either be the way of entry into eternal fellowship with God or He will be the One who is rejected.

Luke records Peter's sermon revealing these truths: *"And he ordered us to preach everywhere and to testify that Jesus is the one appointed ordained by God to be the judge of all—the living and the dead. He is the one all the prophets testified about, saying that everyone who believes in him will have their sins forgiven through his name"* (Acts 10:42-43).

PUTTING IT INTO PRACTICE

Thank God for the ministry of Jesus Christ. Thank Jesus for creating you, redeeming you, and for being a fair and just Judge. Submit to Him. Enter under His authority and seek to become His faithful follower.

Look up and meditate on the following verses: John 5:18; 14:8-9; 20:25-28. Memorize John 1:1-3, 14.

POINTS TO PONDER

- What does it means to be made in the image of God as referred to in Genesis 1?
- What was Christ's role in creation?
- Explain what Jesus' purpose or mission was in becoming flesh?
- Why is it so important we recognize Jesus as God the Son?
- Why is it so significant that Jesus rose from death?

~3~
YOUR SAVIOR

There is salvation in no one else! God has given no other name under heaven by which we must be saved.
— ACTS 4:12

Some people ask, "Saved from what?"

I really do not know any other way to answer what seems to me to be an obvious question but with the obvious answer. We *need* to be saved from death! Haven't you noticed something very consistent about the human condition? Everybody dies.

Remember what we discussed earlier. The best way to learn about our reason for existence is to know God. And we looked at the verse which says God does not die. If our Creator will never die, why then do we die when most of us desire to live?

It is reasonable to suggest that to be made in God's image (Genesis 1:26) would include immortality. Mentally healthy people have a strong desire to live. Even the physically sick want to be healed from their illnesses so they can delay death. We have a longing to live for two reasons: first, our Creator placed this yearning inside of us when He made us. Second, to be made in His image includes reflecting the glory of His immortality.

Yet the fact remains—we all die. God is trying to tell us something; He is warning us of something much more costly and painful than physical demise. He is allowing us to taste of death so we might avoid *eternal* death. We need to be saved from the second death!

How Can We Be Saved From Eternal Death?

Salvation comes through Christ alone.

Immediately, many become anxious when they hear or read such a statement. They are worried for one of three reasons: (1) they are concerned about the feelings and destiny of those who have rejected or have not heard about Christ, (2) they simply disagree because their world view includes spiritual thinking beyond the teachings of the Bible, or (3) they are in a group that finds the discussion of spiritual things irrelevant.

The person and work of Jesus is accepted or included into most of the world religions in one way or another. He is called by some a prophet of God, by others He was a strong and moral leader like India's Gandhi. Some religions even claim that by His life achievements and the grace of God, Jesus ascended into godhood. While it may seem honorable to acknowledge a good man, it is more than dangerous to just lump Jesus in the Spiritual Hall of Fame, many of whom are listed in Hebrews 11. These are great models for us to follow, yet none of them are the Savior of the world. Not one!

Eternal life is given only through the decree and power of Jesus Christ. This was God's plan from the beginning. Salvation from eternal death would require a radical, no-nonsense approach to sin.

Humankind's sin problem has always been too wide for us to cross. Only a plan from the heights and dimensions of heaven could solve the issue of eternal death caused by sin. The Apostle Paul tells the story this way: *"Even before he made the world, God loved us and chose us in Christ to be holy and without fault in his eyes. God decided in advance to adopt us into his own family by bringing us to himself through Jesus Christ. This is what he wanted to do, and it gave him great pleasure. So we praise God for the glorious grace he has poured out on us who belong to his dearly loved Son. He is so rich in kindness and grace that he purchased our freedom with the blood of his Son and forgave our sins"* (Ephesians 1:4-7).

Those who have faith in Christ have been freed from the fear and bondage which comes with sin and death. To have a Savior is to have been rescued and is a cause for rejoicing and unending celebration. It is to realize God cares about you and me. To have a Savior is to have One who *continues* to save us, not only from eternal death, but also from the daily experience of foolishness and selfish living. To have a Savior is to have someone to follow who can be completely trusted.

Salvation comes by grace alone.

You cannot earn God's favor. Salvation is yours through the removal of a death sentence by way of God's forgiving grace. Paul continues his teaching about salvation: *"God saved you by his grace when you believed. And you can't take credit for this; it is a gift from God. Salvation is not a reward for the good things we have done, so none of us can boast about it. For we are God's masterpiece. He has created us anew in Christ Jesus, so that we can do the good things he planned for us long ago"* (Ephesians 2:8-10).

What do these verses tell us beyond the fact that God's salvation is a gift which cannot be earned? We learn that even *believing* is a gift from God. Notice how the verse says *"when you believed."* It does not say *"because* you believed." So how are we saved? It is by God's grace when we believe.

Finally, we also see in verse ten that God's plan of salvation is not just about the destination of heaven, but is about doing the "good things" He has planned for us to do! We will take these things with us to eternity. This is why salvation is both an event and a process. We are once saved, then we are being *continually* saved as we deepen in our awareness and become obedient to the plans God has laid for each of us.

Salvation makes you part of God's family.

To be a Christian is to be an invaluable member of God's family. The house of God in the New Testament is called the Body of Christ. He dwells in us individually and corporately.

This Body of Christ, however, is invisible because it is universal, including both the living and the dead. Therefore it has not yet been finished, but will be, with glorified bodies in the resurrection. But the Body of Christ is also visible through the local church. This is where our

Savior has called us to fellowship and where we discover His presence living in each of us individually and corporately.

Paul explains this further: *"So now you Gentiles are no longer strangers and foreigners. You are citizens along with all of God's holy people. You are members of God's family. Together, we are his house, built on the foundation of the apostles and the prophets. And the cornerstone is Christ Jesus himself. We are carefully joined together in him, becoming a holy temple for the Lord. Through him you Gentiles are also being made part of this dwelling where God lives by his Spirit"* (Ephesians 2:19-22).

God adopted you— and the local church is to *receive* you. In the local Body of Christ is where you will learn to serve and to be served. It is a place where you will discover more about God, others, and yourself. It is not a perfect place but one day it will be. It is this hope and vision which causes us to learn to love like Jesus loved. The local Body of Christ is just like you, with great strengths and abilities, but it also has places of weakness. Jesus is not yet finished with His Body and has not yet completed His work in you. Together we are called to live and serve in community.

Putting it into Practice

Trust in Christ alone for your salvation. If you have not yet humbled yourself to confess with your mouth the belief in your heart that Jesus is truly the only One who can give you life, please take the time to do it now.

Trust in Christ's eternal forgiveness and do not try to make-up for all the wrongs of your life. Instead, follow the way of Christ from this day forward. Relinquish your past, as it can only whisper lies of shame to your present. Let the power of God's forgiveness and the presence of His Spirit guide as you learn how to listen and obey.

Trust in Christ's power to transform the Body of Christ you call home.

Be patient with people the way you would like others to be patient with you. If you do not fellowship in a local Body, find one that teaches the Bible and has a good reputation of consistency in the local community in which it serves. Get involved! Do not be a spectator because you will never grow if you simply listen and do not participate.

POINTS TO PONDER

- Think about the possibility of a God-given instinct to fear death. Why would He do this? What purpose does or would it serve?
- How are we called to serve God?
- Why is belonging to a church so important?
- What must we do to be saved from sin?

~ 4 ~
YOUR COUNSELOR

While Apollos was in Corinth, Paul traveled
through the interior regions until he reached Ephesus,
on the coast, where he found several believers. "Did you
receive the Holy Spirit when you believed?" he
asked them. "No," they replied, "we haven't
even heard that there is a Holy Spirit."
– ACTS 19:1-2

"**Y**ou can't see the forest for the trees."

I do not remember when I first heard this phrase, but I do recall I was young and, at the time, did not understand what it meant. Sometimes life can get so busy and crowded you feel like your wandering aimlessly through the woods. Those who have been lost in the forest say that after awhile everything begins to look the same.

Search and Rescue teams tell us that many people who become disoriented in the woods keep walking in circles, never making progress. And so it is with us. We bury ourselves in tasks, schedules, worries and too many relationships. Eventually, we lose perspective and wander aimlessly.

Like the forest, life is a gorgeous sight when you are looking down upon it from a high place. From the right distance and elevation, life is beautiful—not intimidating, dark or confusing. Instead, it is a masterpiece. Once a person clearly sees the forest and knows how to use a compass, re-entering the trees becomes an adventure of further discovery, not darkness or fear.

Christ sent the Holy Spirit to equip us to follow Him through the forest of life. The Holy Spirit helps you see from the right elevation—from God's perspective. The Spirit helps you navigate through thousands of obstacles, keeping you moving in the right direction. The first two verses in Acts 19 serve as a reminder that it is possible to be a believer yet unaware of the importance of knowing the Holy Spirit. These disciples were God "fearers," but had never been introduced to the person of the Holy Spirit.

WHAT DOES GOD THE SPIRIT DO?

The Holy Spirit is your Counselor.

When Jesus told His followers that He would soon leave to go back to the Father, they were obviously concerned. He was their strength and hope—their teacher and they all knew of His love on a first-hand basis. Sensing their concern, Jesus made two important facts clear. He would return someday to finish God's redemptive plans and He would send God the Holy Spirit.

Jesus declared, *"If you love me, you will obey what I command. And I will ask the Father, and he will give you another Counselor to be with you forever—the Spirit of truth. The world cannot accept him, because it neither sees him nor knows him. But you know him, for he lives with you and will be in you"* (John 14:15-17 NIV).

Love for God is a desire to know Him and be like Him. But this is impossible in our own strength. He must reveal Himself to us, teach and empower us to understand and obey.

The Spirit is called Counselor because He helps us as only God can—revealing the truth of Scripture. The Holy Spirit never contradicts the Bible because He was the divine influence ruling within the human authors. The Spirit has always been present among us but as a believer, He now resides within your very being. You are the house He lives in. He is not a mist or a force; He is God living in each believer. He can do this because He is omnipresent; everywhere all the time.

What makes His presence effective in you rather than an unbeliever is your willingness to give up control of your life to Him. You recognize the nearness of God because He speaks to your heart and mind. You were once dead or deaf to God but now you are alive to Him and can hear His voice. The Spirit in you is your most rewarding relationship on earth.

The Holy Spirit is God's mark on your life.

His presence is God's seal of ownership, and His ruling in you is your guarantee of eternal life. He is the transforming power which continues to create in you the person of Jesus Christ. The Apostle Paul explains: *"The Spirit is God's guarantee that he will give us the inheritance he promised and that he has purchased us to be his own people. He did this so we would praise and glorify him"* (Ephesians 1:14).

This verse reminds us what we have learned earlier: we cannot do anything to earn God's favor. Salvation and sanctification are the result of God's power, not ours. Sanctification is the promise of God to set us apart as a people to Himself. It is the ongoing process of salvation. This is why we say, "We have been saved, we are being saved, and we will be saved."

Yes, it is true that believers want to please God and accomplish His pleasure. However, we cannot lose sight of the fact that even our desire and ability to please Him comes from Him alone. A spiritually near-sighted person can only see the personal accomplishments, but cannot see well enough to thank God for giving the desire and the ability in the first place. It is the Spirit working in us that reminds us to Whom we belong—and this is cause for great joy.

The Holy Spirit is Christ alive in you.

The Spirit of God is sometimes called the Spirit of Christ because the Spirit always honors the person and ministry of Christ. Jesus said of the Spirit, *"He will bring me glory by telling you whatever he receives from me"* (John 16:14).

Because Christ is the living model for us to imitate, the Spirit continues to encourage us to follow in His ways. As the apostle Paul explains, *"But you are not controlled by your sinful nature. You are controlled by the Spirit if you have the Spirit of God living in you. (And remember that those who do not have the Spirit of Christ living in them do not belong to him at all)"* (Romans 8:9).

Paul's words are powerful. As a believer, to be controlled by the sinful nature is not normal, but it is standard Christian behavior to be controlled by the Spirit. To act in sinful patterns requires deliberate acts of rebellion.

There is a difference between human weakness and the sinful nature. Our human weakness is the reality that we have the ability to sin, the experience of being tired and hungry. It is the reality of dependence; we require certain conditions to survive. The knowledge we can get sick and die; that the chemical make-up of our bodies can create many challenges; that our childhood still impacts us today. All these are human weaknesses.

The sinful nature exists beyond the realm of human weakness. It is devious and dark and seeks to please itself at the expense of all others. It cannot be trusted and is consistently evil in all thoughts and actions. When the sinful nature is not restrained in the life of a person by the grace of God, there is no limit to its potential damage to self and others. It is what brings about great evils and false teaching.

In the believer, however, the sinful nature no longer has power over the new creation of God within. The apostle John writes: *"But you belong to God, my dear children. You have already won a victory over those people, because the Spirit who lives in you is greater than the spirit who lives in the world"* (1 John 4:4-5).

To obey the sinful nature is to consciously and willingly choose to accept the carnal things and darkness over the voice and power of the Spirit—and what is good.

PUTTING IT INTO PRACTICE

Being filled with the Holy Spirit is to be directed and empowered by Him. Consciously, by choice, be dependent upon the Spirit in all manners of life.

To be filled by God's Spirit is to surrender every area to Him. It requires you to turn away from your own methods and sin and reach out to God. One of the best teachings in Scripture on becoming dependent upon Christ is found in John 15:1-8.

Read this text and imagine yourself as a branch connected to a vine (Jesus). Realize the implication. Everything you need for sustenance flows from the vine, and in order to bear fruit, you must remain connected.

After you read the Scripture, make a list of the things in your life where you have not relied upon Christ. Then ask Him to give you the faith to trust Him for these things. If you make this a habit, you will begin to experience a daily relationship with the Spirit of Christ.

POINTS TO PONDER

- Why did the Holy Spirit come?
- What does it mean to be "filled" with the Holy Spirit?
- What does He produce in you as a result of "filling"?
- Why is the average Christian not filled with the Holy Spirit?
- According to Scripture, what is the difference between human weakness and sinful nature?

~ 5 ~
YOUR FATHER

*But to all who believed him and accepted him, he
gave the right to become children of God. They are
reborn—not with a physical birth resulting from human
passion or plan, but a birth that comes from God.*
—JOHN 1:12-13 (NLT)

Many Christian psychologists have suggested that people have a tendency to view God and other authority figures in light of their own fathers. Our relational experience with our earthly father is the birthplace of understanding all other authoritative sources. In other words, our relationship with our father is the magnifying glass we look through as we focus on our Heavenly Father. For some of us this is good news and for others it is potentially bad. One thing is certain—nobody has experienced a perfect earthly father.

I am one of the fortunate ones. Though my father proved his imperfections throughout my life, he was a good man. My dad was consistent, hard-working, forgiving and playful. He respected authority and taught me about discipline and the things of God. And he has always been faithful to mom. So how do I typically view God? Without hesitation and without a complete review of my orthodoxy, I know God to be strong, unmoving yet accepting and forgiving.

To me, the Almighty is tough; not mean but tough. He is a tower of strength. He does not crush me, but I cannot move or manipulate Him. God is God! I have found that He does not do things the way I want or as fast as I would like, yet He alone knows what is best.

My weak human emotions and finite understanding often hates what God will or will not do on my behalf. On the other hand, my Heavenly

Father is accepting and forgiving. He knows my strength is nothing like His, and that I do not know what I need. He understands that my weaknesses can cause me to sin. In fact, He knows me better than I know myself!

Because God is like an unmovable mountain of consistency, I can hide in Him and be sheltered by His generosity and wisdom. My life therefore is hidden in the character and strength of an unshakable yet merciful God. So no matter what trouble visits me, I can be strengthened by the Father. I can run to Him and find shelter in the midst of storms.

I have no enemy that can penetrate the mountain of God. There exists no special force which can snatch me away from His hiding place. If He is stern with me, He is tougher on those who hate me. If He is merciful to me, He can be merciful to *anyone*. This is how I view God the Father.

How Does Relating to God as Your Heavenly Father Transform You?

Knowing God as your Father will change your perspective on life.

To believe you are a son or daughter of the greatest Father who will ever exist alters the way you view your circumstances. No matter how bad it may feel at times, you know your life is still a gift, because to never be born only means to never live. What we experience on earth will one day come to an end and eternity, without the decaying affects of sin, is on the horizon.

Your Father in Heaven chose to bring you into the world to experience its good and its bad—so you might long for what is good and desire to spend forever with Him. Life may not be perfect from our vantage point; however, God's eternal plan is without flaws; perfect because He is perfect.

We all experience anxiety because we cannot see as God sees. So much is uncertain since we don't know the future. Yet, the Father is not anxious about you because He is perfect—and His love is greater than

His most evil enemy.

To bring this into focus, Jesus tells us to be just like the Father in His perfection: *"If you love only those who love you, what reward is there for that? Even corrupt tax collectors do that much. If you are kind only to your friends, how are you different from anyone else? Even pagans do that. But you are to be perfect, even as your Father in heaven is perfect"* (Matthew 5:46-48).

Jesus' teachings may seem harsh, but they provide insight into the Father. His love for us is stronger than our inability to love Him back with the same measure. And it is so powerful, He expects us to love the same way He loves.

However, God would not expect us to do something He has not given us the ability to accomplish. Because of His love for us, we have the ability to love all people, regardless of how they have hurt us. One dimension of perfection is to love your enemies: to pray for and be kind to them. We can do this because God the Father deeply cares for us. To know you are loved by the Lord provides power to overcome the smaller and weaker human impulses.

Knowing God as your Father will change your view of Him.

Some people are afraid of the Almighty, as if He was like the abusive fathers they have known here on earth. As a result, these individuals hide from God. Some attempt to make deals with Him, trying to avoid a problem or to gain something desired. Others view Him as the "big genie" in the sky. Still others see Him as absent—because that's how they experienced their earthly father.

Thankfully, many view Him as caring. All of these mental pictures of God reflect life's experiences and deep hidden emotions.

Like good parents, the Heavenly Father has a consistent and balanced approach to raising children toward maturity. Here's how James describes the Father looking at our lives: *"Whatever is good and perfect comes down to us from God our Father, who created all the lights in the heavens. He never changes or casts a shifting shadows. He chose to give birth to us by giving us his true word, And we, out of all creation, became his prized possession"* (James 1:17-18).

We are treasured by God, and His word does not change. He is not like a star that burns out of the sky. When God says something, you can count on it. He does not get distracted and He is never overwhelmed. He is not trying to ruin anyone's hopes, nor is He worried whether you like Him or not. Your Father is always available and He welcomes your fellowship—conversation, thanks, praise, concerns and needs.

Knowing God as your Father will change your view of family.

Some families grow stronger over time, while others seem to fall apart. What determines the destiny of a family more than any other factors is the love and stability of the mothers and dads. Parents teach us what we need—and what we can do without. They instruct us in what is right and wrong, and demonstrate strength or weakness during times of difficulty.

Kids from great homes learn safety, contentment and trust, while those raised in environments of chaos often become people filled with anger and anxiety.

Jesus teaches us what it is like to be a child of the Heavenly Father: Speaking about the worries over our basic needs, He says,

"These things dominate the thoughts of unbelievers, but your heavenly Father already knows all your needs. Seek the Kingdom of God above all else, and live righteously, and he will give you everything you need. So don't worry about tomorrow, for tomorrow will bring its own worries. Today's trouble is enough for today" (Matthew 6:32-34).

In this example, pagans are likened to kids growing up in a hostile home filled with everything but love. The result is a sense of survival. On the other hand, we get a glimpse of what it means to be a child of God. He already knows our needs even before we ask.

The family of God works like this: when we care about the things God cares about, the rest will fall into place. This is God's promise. Then He instructs as a caring and wise Father, reminding us not to waste our concerns on what lies ahead. Today is our opportunity to live as one of God's children. Tomorrow is in His hands.

PUTTING IT INTO PRACTICE

Relate to God as your Heavenly Father. In fact, when you pray, address Him as "Father." Read Matthew 6:9-13 and pray as Jesus instructs. But remember, He is not saying that the words of the Lord's Prayer are the only way to pray. He is emphasizing relating to God as "Our Father"— the only One who can meet your needs and the One you should trust.

The second thing I want you to do is to identify the experiences (or lack of) you encountered with your earthly father that could be creating problems in understanding how God feels about you. Perhaps you will share these with a mature believer who is willing to discuss and help you discover a rewarding relationship with God.

If your earthly father was great, praise and thank him if he is living. If he was not the best dad, try to remember there is probably more to his story than you know or can comprehend. Love him and thank God for him because without your father, you would not exist.

POINTS TO PONDER

- How does knowing God as your Father change your view of family?
- How would you characterize your earthly father? How does this view of your father compare with your perception of Father God?
- Have you ever been angry with the Lord? If so, does this make you feel guilty?
- Since we are to care about what God cares about, what do you believe these things are?

~ 6 ~
YOUR LORD

*"Teacher, which is the most important
commandment in the law of Moses?" Jesus
replied, "You must love the Lord your God with
all your heart, all your soul, and all your mind. This is
the first and greatest commandment. A second is equally
important: 'Love your neighbor as yourself.' All the other
commandments and all the demands of the prophets
are based on these two commandments."*
– MATTHEW 22:36-40

I was sitting next to the hospital bed of my nine year old son who was fighting for his life. Out of nowhere some sort of post-strep virus aggressively attacked both of his kidneys. I was waiting for the doctor and his team to come and give us the final action plan—looking for a clear answer that would save his young life.

Just months earlier, my friend and pastor Dan Vasquez died with Melanoma cancer at the age of 43. We prayed and fasted for his healing as he went through surgeries and cancer fighting treatments. For nine months we fought alongside of him and his family. The physical battle was lost, which didn't make any sense. He was energetic and faithful, a good and godly man as well as a pastor to his people. We asked the Lord politely, we asked in confidence and faith, and we asked Him in desperation. God simply and quietly said "no."

To say the least, the confidence I had to see my son walk out of that hospital was not a testimony of faith which would inspire a great story. I was tired in ministry and was weary of hearing God say no. Like a self-fulfilling prophecy, the medical team pulled me aside and the lead physician delivered the news. My son's chances of survival were slim. We were told to brace ourselves for the worst.

Several minutes later I found myself walking down the hallways of the hospital telling God exactly what I thought about His unmovable self. I told Him it really didn't matter what I desired because He was going to do whatever He wanted. He was the boss and I was just a servant begging for the scraps off His table.

During a short break from my arrogance and irreverence, I cried, "Lord, please do not take my son away." Then, when I came back to my typical transparent self, I told the Lord that if He did take my son, I would not at all be pleased. However, I assured God I would still serve Him, even if He took my boy. What a relief that must have been for the Lord! I'm sure He was really nervous about losing my contributions to His ministry on earth!

At some point during the day I built up enough courage to keep my promise and tell my son what the doctors had told me. However, my son knew something I didn't. After sharing the bad news, this nine year-old boy looked at his dad lying next to him in bed and said, "Dad, this disease is Goliath, but I am David."

I had to leave the room before he saw me break into tears of confused emotions.

Just a few days later, we all walked out of the hospital together as a family. It took a couple of years for him to get back to his old self, but they went by like a cool breeze on a warm day.

What I learned through the human tragedy of losing my pastor and friend while receiving back my son was the Lordship of Jesus Christ. Sometimes He gives and sometimes He takes way. But even in the taking, He gives—though we do not always recognize this. If I love anything or anyone more than I love God, I will only grow disappointed, frustrated, and bitter.

WHAT DOES IT MEAN FOR CHRIST TO BE OUR LORD?

God's greatest commandment is Him: to learn of Him, to know Him, and to love Him.

Jesus makes this clear as He says, *"'You must love the Lord your God with all your heart, all your soul, and all your mind.' This is the first and greatest commandment"* (Matthew 22:37-38).

God wants to be the very center of your life. He is not looking to be the first priority on a task list of daily duties, rather He desires to be right in the middle of every thought and deed. After-all, the Lord constantly thinks of you. Psalm 139:17-18 speaks to the fact that your Father, God, Lord, and Master finds continual joy in His thoughts toward you: *"How precious are your thoughts about me, O God. They cannot be numbered! I can't even count them; they outnumber the grains of sand! And when I wake up, you are still with me!"*

When we find ourselves in the midst of trouble, we can begin to believe the Lord is too busy, or He doesn't care. These verses, however, teach us the opposite.

The only reason we sometimes think God isn't concerned is when we love someone or something more than Him. As our Lord, He is all we need.

Here's where we get confused. Because He loves us, He often blesses us with the people and things we enjoy. Then we begin to love the blessings more than the One who blesses. To make Jesus Christ our Lord, we must come to the place where we are willing to live with great gain or great loss, because both fade in comparison to the eternal joy of knowing the Lord of the universe.

As the apostle Paul began to appreciate the Lordship of Christ, he began to view his circumstances differently. Let's look at his testimony: *"...for I have learned how to be content with whatever I have. I know how to live on almost nothing or with everything. I have learned the secret of living in every situation, whether it is with a full stomach or empty, with plenty or little. For I can do everything through Christ, who gives me strength"* (Philippians 4:11-13).

This is easier said than done. However, Paul can say it because he *lived* it. Notice how Paul does not say having much (or little) is wrong or immoral. His statement is clear. We can be content in *any* circumstance because the Lord makes us strong in every situation.

The Lord's greatest commandments are relational.

The Lordship of Jesus Christ is not about Him being a bully. Frankly, it is His mercy which keeps us alive. He is not concerned about impressing us, because He knows who He is. The Triune God lives in perfect harmony and unity, and everything that comes from Him is for the same purpose—relational perfection. In other words, nothing matters more to God than right relationships.

The Ten Commandments are a great example of God's relational theme. The first four commandments deal primarily with having a right relationship with the Almighty: worship no other god, do not have idols, do not misuse the Lord's name, and set one day aside each week just for remembering Him. The remaining six deal with having a right relationship with others: honor your parents, do not murder, do not commit adultery, do not steal, do not be a false witness, and do not covet the possessions of others.

In the New Testament, Jesus summarizes all the moral law and ethics into two relational thoughts: love God and love others (Matthew 22:37-40).

The Father's greatest concern for those who are not in a right relationship with Him and others is reconciliation. If you break a bone in your body, all your priorities change. It really doesn't matter what appointment you miss because your mind and body demand the bone be set back in place—this is the desire of reconciliation. If you really want to know the Lord and be part of His Kingdom, fellowship with Him must be your central concern. If your link to another is broken, your priorities must change.

To have Jesus Christ as your Lord requires that you seek to live at peace with everyone. As Paul explains: *"Never pay back evil with more evil. Do things in such a way that everyone can see you are honorable. Do all that you can to live in peace with everyone"* (Romans 12:17-18).

To know God as the Lord of your life is to be in the people business. Your personality type isn't the issue. Some of us are more naturally people oriented and others are more tasks oriented, but we were all made to relate.

PUTTING IT INTO PRACTICE

We must love God more than anything or anyone else. Only heartache and confusion await those who desire the mercy of God without the Lordship of Jesus Christ. Jesus is Lord of *all* things— regardless of whether or not we recognize Him as so in our daily lives. To live under His authority requires us to be willing to do whatever He asks. Simply put, He is the boss.

To help you in this process, memorize Matthew 22:36-40 and Philippians 2:11. Then begin to identify the areas in your life where you have not made Jesus Lord. Make a commitment to give these to Christ.

POINTS TO PONDER

- What is God's greatest commandments to us as believers?
- Read Philippians 4:11-13 out loud. What struggles do you have relating to this truth?
- How can we hold each other accountable in this area of loving the blessings more than the Giver of these blessings?

~ 7 ~
GOD IS IN CONTROL

The Lord works out everything for his own ends
—even the wicked for a day of disaster.
– PROVERBS 16:4 (NIV)

I would be a liar if I said losing doesn't bother me. I'm not sure I can explain why. Perhaps it's because I am the first-born child of four; or maybe because I am short in stature and have a chip on my soul. And I'm sure having to overcome first impressions on the court of athletics due to my size has contributed to my bend toward competitiveness. Sometimes this trait has helped me, and sometimes it has hurt. It helps when I need to persevere and persist in noble activities. It hurts when I take myself too seriously or when I believe I can change things that only God can change.

It was 9:50 A.M. I was sitting alone in a chair on the front row in a small, carpeted elementary school gymnasium. We had about 150 chairs set-up for the grand opening service of a brand new church we were starting in a Denver suburb. We had moved from California to Colorado with very few contacts.

By the time we were ready to start the new church we were just a small group of people—about 30 in number including the children. We prayed, planned and worked hard inviting the unchurched community to try out a new ministry designed for those who had experienced little of church and didn't know much about the God of Christianity.

Ten minutes before the "grand" opening, no one other than a few of the faithful core team members were present. Thoughts of personal failure began to invade the attitude of my mind. In those few minutes before the service, I began to examine my motives for starting this new church. I went through this exercise because I knew I had a history of trying to prove myself to myself—to others, and maybe even to the Lord—that I was a valuable member of God's creation. An over-competitive person is an insecure person. However, to my surprise, I was sincerely able to conclude that this church plant was started with the intention of being faithful to God—nothing more and nothing less. At that moment new thoughts entered my mind.

I began to smile inside and it worked itself onto my face. I reminded myself that this is God's work, not Jim's work. I did my part to the best of my ability and knowledge. The rest was up to the Lord, and I was at peace with these thoughts. If the church plant failed it was a great run and I learned much from the experience. By the way, five minutes past the hour nearly 200 people came through the doors and some of them helped us set up extra chairs!

How Do We Know Christ Is In Control?

God is good and life is good.

To believe otherwise is a sign of a discouraged mind. God is good because He created life from His own being. He made us when we were nothing.

Let's get practical for a moment. If you can, try to make your theology as simple as possible. When time is short, this is what I tell people who want to know about my thoughts on what we don't comprehend: "I believe God is good, I believe He will do what is right, and I can trust Him with the things I can not comprehend."

What are the subjects of life we do not understand? These are the ones I hear the most: Why do good people die young? Why is there so much pain in the world? How can God send a person to a place of suffering for eternity?

Some of these concerns can be answered logically by our theology. For example, it makes sense to me that if God wanted to give His creation an opportunity to experience fellowship with Him, He had to give that creation a choice to do so. To force His creation to love would not be love at all, but merely manipulation.

The result of choice is sometimes good and often otherwise. This is a short but simple answer to the pain we experience. This explanation however, does not clarify why one child dies and another does not. We have no answers, but we use the one we sometimes like and sometimes dislike—God is in control.

Then there is the question of eternal damnation. If a person lives a horrible and corrupt life for fifty years in full view of the consequences, is it just for God to sentence him to Hell for eternity? Good question. Various spheres of Christianity have offered doctrines which provide some comfort to the human mind, but these teachings are difficult at best to defend from a scriptural world view.

As humans, we generally do not like it when certain things don't make sense to us. They frustrate and anger us to the point where we will even fight among ourselves and argue about situations none of us have experienced or have control over.

The Bible speaks of an eternal place of suffering and separation from God called Hell, or eternal fire. This place was created for evil spiritual beings, but Jesus also made reference to people being sent there: *"Then the King will turn to those on the left and say, 'Away with you, you cursed ones, into the eternal fire prepared for the devil and his demons"* (Matthew 25:41-42).

I once heard a wise teacher say, "The Bible does not tell us everything we may want to know, it tells us everything we *need* to know." In other words, we are on a "need to know" basis. It may not sound very relational, yet then again we must remember Who creates and who is created.

Sin is contained.

On occasions we have a difficult time realizing it, but the mercy of God is restraining sin from destroying us completely. Again, God is in control. Many believers focus on the wrong enemy. They zero in on people, their opinions, personalities and even their aggression against the things of God.

41

While we know evil people exist, Scripture teaches us that the war we sense is not with people: *"Be strong in the Lord and in his mighty power. Put on all of God's armor so that you will be able to stand firm against all strategies of the devil. For we are not fighting against flesh-and-blood enemies, but against evil rulers and authorities of the unseen world, against mighty powers in this dark world, and against evil spirits in the heavenly places"* (Ephesians 6:10-12).

A question remains: Why does God hold back evil; why not bring His people home and destroy evil once and for all and be done with it? The Lord is patient with us and knows many more will trust Him and come to Him. This is why God holds back evil, so He can accept more people into His family.

Notice the apostle Peter's teaching on this matter: *"The Lord isn't really being slow about his promise, as some people think. No, he is being patient for your sake. He does not want anyone to be destroyed, but wants everyone to repent"* (2 Peter 3:9).

Here again, God's reasoning is relational. To know the Father and to love Him would cause a person to care about the things He cares about—people. God is good and life is good because of the opportunities He provides. This is why He sustains life.

Justice is imminent.

The Almighty is certainly in control and our free choices will be brought into accountability. Though God is patient, the Day of Judgment will come. Peter continues his discourse on the end times: *"But the day of the Lord will come as unexpectedly as a thief. Then the heavens will pass away with a terrible noise, and the very elements themselves will disappear in fire, and the earth and everything on it will be found to deserve judgment. Since everything around us is going to be destroyed like this, what holy and godly lives you should live, looking forward to the day of God and hurrying it along. On that day, he will set the heavens on fire, and the elements will melt away in the flames. But we are looking forward to the new heavens and new earth he has promised, a world filled with God's righteousness"* (2 Peter 3:10-13).

For the believer, this is a great time. Evil will be dealt with and justice will be served. Those who belong to God through faith in Jesus Christ will live in a new place sometimes called heaven and described here as "the new heavens and new earth." We will get a new beginning that will never end, and it will be free of the dangers and destruction of our sin.

Perhaps you find yourself wondering if you can continue to live a life free from iniquity. Or perhaps the thought of judgment makes you fearful. Once more, God is in control. He has pledged He will not allow a temptation to come into your life that you cannot defeat with His help. Notice this promise in Paul's letter to the church in Corinth: *"If you think you are standing strong, be careful not to fall. The temptations in your life are no different from what others experience. And God is faithful. He will not allow the temptation to be more than you can stand. When you are tempted, he will show you a way out so that you can endure"* (1 Corinthians 10:12-13).

If we have wandered away from Him and His people, we typically fall prey to the temptations that surround us. A common enticement is to focus on the differences humans invent in regard to religious traditions, styles and non-essentials.

God is less concerned about the various denominations of Christianity than we are. He does desire unity under one banner, but the banner is not the name of a church or a religion. He wants all believers to unite under the person of Jesus Christ. Paul explains how this has always been the Father's plan: *"God's purpose in all this was to use the church to display his wisdom in its rich variety to all the unseen rulers and authorities in the heavenly places. This was his eternal plan, which he carried out through Christ Jesus our Lord"* (Ephesians 3:10-11).

PUTTING IT INTO PRACTICE

Trust God. Do not fret over world events, but know He is in control. Do not trust Him to do what you want, trust Him to do what is right. The best way to begin this new habit is to list the things going on in your life, family, community and the world that you are anxious about or dislike. Then ask yourself this question: "Is this something God wants me to address or is this something He wants me to hand over to Him in faith?"

POINTS TO PONDER

- Explain how God is in control of all things even though we have free-will.
- Why do you think so many Christians still crumble in the face of evil temptation?
- Are there areas of your life in which you need to examine your intentions? Is God fully using you, or do you still try to run the show and resist Him?
- How hard must you work to get into heaven?

~ 8 ~
GOD'S PERFECTION

*It was in the year King Uzziah died that I
saw the Lord. He was sitting on a lofty throne, and
the train of his robe filled the Temple. Attending him
were mighty seraphim, each having six wings. With two wings
they covered their faces, with two they covered their feet, and
with two they flew. They were calling out to each other, "Holy,
holy, holy is the Lord of Heavens Armies! The whole earth is
filled with his glory!" Their voices shook the Temple to its
foundations, and the entire building was filled with smoke.*

— ISAIAH 6:1-4

Practically every competition I have participated in and those I can
think of is graded on the curve. To win a game, one need not be perfect.
He or she just needs to be better than the opposing player. For example,
there has never been a baseball player who hit on average of 1,000 in any
one season. Even if one were to accomplish such a feat, was every hit a
home run? Did he ever swing and miss? I'm sure you get the point.

Competition is not about perfection, rather about being better than
your opponent. When a person establishes a new high mark of
performance, we label it as "a new record." The new mark stands until
someone else comes along and improves on the previous
accomplishment.

This is the world we live in; the human experience. Unfortunately,
it is built into the way we think. Who is the smartest, the nicest, the best
this or that? It also impacts the way we view God. To many, it seems
logical that whoever has lived the best life according to God's standards
would be the one person guaranteed entrance into heaven—and by

whom we all will be compared. Perhaps this is why we often size ourselves up with others. Sometimes this makes us feel better, or it reveals great shortcomings.

I wish we did not view our faith and standing before God the same way we experience sports, school, relationships, money and achievements. Faith is not a competition of piety, nor is it a sport where the best spiritual athlete wins. These ideas insult the holiness of God. There is only One who is perfect and there is only one definition of perfection—God. Even if you are the best person who has ever lived, this is of no use to Him. You are no further ahead than anyone else.

What Does it Mean to Say "God is Perfect"?

Nothing and no one is a threat to God.

He is eternal—always existing and the definition of perfection. Some say Satan and God are at war. Those who believe this forget something important. The created is no threat to the Creator. Satan is a fallen angel and is a pawn in the hands of the Almighty. If there is a war, Satan has declared it but there is nothing but peace in God's home.

Apparently, the Lord even transcends heaven: *"Then there was war in heaven. Michael and his angels fought against the dragon and his angels. And the dragon lost the battle, and he and his angels were forced out of heaven. This great dragon—the ancient serpent called the devil, or Satan, the one deceiving the whole world—was thrown down to the earth with all his angels"* (Revelation 12:7-9).

These verses tell the classic story of good versus evil, yet do not suggest in any way that God's throne was in jeopardy.

God is the definition of all that can be defined as good.

Anything you can find that is good comes from God. Everything He made is filled with beauty and excellence, reflecting His perfection. The angels worshiping God in Isaiah's vision declare this truth, *"Holy, holy, holy is the Lord Almighty! The whole earth is filled with his glory!"*

For the believer, there is a bright side to the darkest events of our lives. No matter how ugly and painful life can be, God's perfection has a way of making it good. Sometimes He accomplishes this during our lifetime and sometimes after. Paul writes concerning this truth: *"...the Holy Spirit helps us in our weakness. For example, we don't know what God wants us to pray for. But the Holy Spirit prays for us with groanings that cannot be expressed in words. And the Father who knows all hearts knows what the Spirit is saying, for the Spirit pleads for us believers in harmony with God's own will. And we know that God causes everything to work together for the good of those who love God and are called according to his purpose for them"* (Romans 8:26-28).

When we as believers are distressed and turn to God in prayer we often don't know what to say other than, "Please stop the pain." However, our limited understanding and spiritual vocabulary does not stop the Lord from hearing our hearts. The Spirit of God translates our troubles into heavenly language. Then our holy God continues His process of perfecting us and making us like His Son. He causes all things to work together perfectly according to His plan. While on earth, our view of perfection and His can be quite different; nonetheless, His ways are perfect even dealing with us as sinners.

All of God's attributes flow from His perfection—His holiness.

God is not moody; He is consistent. If He gives mercy it is also just—and if He brings to your life discipline, He is also providing you with wisdom. The Father's attributes are not like a craftsmen's workshop where some tools are in need of repair. They are all perfect. One is not in service while others lie on the work bench. They are all dynamic never lying dormant.

The various words or phrases we use to describe His attributes come from the same divine well—His perfection.

God is Sovereign • *God is Eternal* • *God is All-Knowing*
• *God is Ever-Present* • *God is All-Powerful* • *God Never Changes*
• *God is Righteous* • *God is Just* • *God is Love* • *God is Truth*

You have two ways to respond to this. You can have a flippant attitude which says, "Leave me alone, I'm not Jesus Christ!" Or you can do what Isaiah did as he embraced the perfection of God. He immediately humbled himself by saying, "Now that I see perfection, I know that I am a man who is far from God and I live among a people in the same condition."

Then Isaiah declared, *"It's all over! I am doomed, for I am a sinful man. I have filthy lips, and I live among a people with filthy lips. Yet I have seen the King, the Lord of Heaven's Armies"* (Isaiah 6:5).

Do you notice the difference? Our attitude can use the perfection of God as an excuse, while Isaiah sees the holiness of God and is amazed and humbled by the immeasurable gap which separates him from the Father.

In the same way, there are two kinds of people: those who fellowship with individuals they view as "less than themselves." This evidently makes them feel more acceptable in a competitive world. Then there are those who desire to learn from others who are further down the road in their spiritual growth. These people know they need help and strive to become more like Christ.

Read more of Isaiah's story: *"Then one of the seraphim flew to me with a burning coal he had taken from the altar with a pair of tongs. He touched my lips with it and said, 'See, this coal has touched your lips. Now your guilt is removed, and your sins are forgiven.' Then I heard the Lord asking, 'Whom should I send as a messenger to this people? Who will go for us?' I said, 'Here I am. Send me'"* (Isaiah 6:6-8).

Which are you? Are you flippant about the gap between you and God or are you drawn in as a worshiper and ready to respond as the Spirit leads?

PUTTING IT INTO PRACTICE

Worship God for He is perfection. Many of us have no clue what the Lord has for us because we are not worshipers. As we come before Him, He will direct and guide us for His purposes and in His ways. Gather with believers and voice back to God His attributes. If this is not possible, get alone with God and praise Him, or write His virtues in a journal as a prayer of praise to the Lord.

You can worship Him in spirit and truth as you write or say aloud such things as: "Father, I praise You because You never change. You are the same today, yesterday and forever. I praise You because You know all things. Your thoughts are beyond me. Thank You for making me and loving me."

The more you make this a habit, the more you will gain confidence in the fact God is good and He is in control.

POINTS TO PONDER

- Why is God's mighty throne never in jeopardy to Satan?
- Why is God never threatened by heavenly battles or spiritual warfare?
- What are some of the ways we see God's perfection in creation of things on earth (e.g. the form of a new flower, the ability of the human eye, the rotation of the planets, etc...)? Enjoy these pictures and reflect on the perfection of God by examining these things. Celebrate them.

~ 9 ~
YOUR STRENGTH

My health may fail, and my spirit may grow weak, but
God remains the strength of my heart; he is mine forever.
— PSALM 73:26

We were heading down the highway at 60 miles per hour in my green 1971 Cougar. I was sitting in the passenger seat and my fiancé was behind the wheel. I had only a split second or two to speak and my words were few and to the point: "Lord, here I come." There was no middle divider that separated the north bound lane from the south bound. A white van crossed over the middle line and hit us nearly head-on.

The next thing I can remember is waking up to a voice asking, "Are you alright?" The police, fire department, ambulance and witnesses were on the scene before I awoke from unconsciousness. I looked over to see if my best friend in the whole world was still alive. Her head was leaning up against the steering wheel, her eyes closed, and the blood dripping from her face puddled in her lap.

Both of us were badly hurt, but thank God we survived. In those days, very few people wore seat belts. If it wasn't for the Cougar's long hood that covered that big 351 Cleveland engine inside, I don't think we would have made it. Our injuries included a separated shoulder, a collapsed lung, stitches, bumps and bruises.

My fiancé—now my wife—was most upset because this accident happened just weeks before our wedding. Fortunately, all the noticeable evidences of our collision could be hidden from the eye of the camera on our wedding day!

The drunk driver who crossed over the line and his passengers were enjoying a night of meaningless euphoria. We were heading back home after spending a day at church and recreation with family and friends. I was twenty years old and my final words were "Lord, here I come!"

I've spent many hours reflecting upon that event and the words which bubbled up from my soul. Lord knows, I was not a candidate for the priesthood. I knew the Lord and spoke with Him often but I was very much like many twenty year old men. I was full of myself.

My last words were not just a confession of faith; they were etched upon my heart. They reflected my true DNA. Though not yet fully realized, I knew deep down that my only real purpose for existence was found in God. My reason for being was not my vocation, my gifts or my dreams; it was in my destiny.

I knew that if I died, I would find myself in a new reality. I would be in the conscious presence of God without the sins of my past or the shortcomings of my flesh. My strength, and yours, rests in His hands.

HOW DOES CHRIST PROVIDE STRENGTH?

Christ provides strength by giving us an eternal perspective.

When all my energy is gone, I still have confidence in the strength God provides through Christ. Though I had no power to stop the imminent collision that day, I was able to borrow from a divine resource. I was ready to go to God and I had no doubt He was waiting to receive me.

At the age of twenty, I was not yet looking forward to Heaven but I knew in those few seconds I was going home to my Heavenly Father. I knew my entrance into God's house was not based upon my merit or my penance. It was only due to the faith God gave me in the person and ministry of Jesus Christ. I have strength which doesn't come from me, but from Christ.

Christ provides the desire to grow and finish strong.

The longer you walk with God the more you begin to realize you are alive for a purpose. Yes, I was in an automobile accident that should have taken my life, yet I truly believe it was not an accident that I lived through it. God's purposes would have been accomplished on that day whether I lived or died.

Once you acquire the strength and desire to grow and finish your life strong, you will need some coaching on what this objective requires of you. It's often not what you think. For example, the new Christian often feels anxiousness to do something great for the Kingdom of God. The problem with this kind of thinking is that it tends to tell the Almighty what to do instead of getting our direction from heaven.

In God's Kingdom there is a different economy of greatness. It is achieved by joyfully and willingly doing whatever the Lord requires. In the words of Jesus: *"Whoever wants to be a leader among you must be your servant, and whoever wants to be first among you must become your slave. For even the Son of Man came not to be served but to serve others and to give his life as a ransom for many"* (Matthew 20:26-28).

This is another paradox. To be great in God's Kingdom is to become excellent at serving. However, we cannot successfully serve God and sinful humanity without the strength of Christ. When we serve in our own power, we tend to look for quiet appreciation or sometimes public recognition. To grow is to become a *better* servant; to finish strong is to die an *excellent* servant.

Christ is your reward.

The reason we often look for an incentive is because we cannot fathom the joy of eternity in a Kingdom ruled by Christ and absent from sin. The New Testament tells us that awards will be given in heaven; however, our greatest reward is Christ. His strength resurrects and glorifies our body giving us the gift of immortality. Our motivation should come from our longing to see Christ's Kingdom fully established once and for all.

Here's the amazing thing about strength, growth, finishing strong and reward: Christ is the one who accomplishes it in us, yet He shares the glory with us as we live for Him. As Paul writes, *"...I am certain that God, who began the good work within you, will continue his work until it is finally finished on the day when Christ Jesus returns"* (Philippians 1:6).

From the pages of the Bible, it is clear that Christ does everything He can to help us live successful and meaningful lives. The only things that can frustrate His grace are the conscious and willful choices to repeatedly disobey. The Word warns about not cooperating with God's grace: *"And do not bring sorrow to God's Holy Spirit by the way you live. Remember, he has identified you as his own, guaranteeing that you will be saved on the day of redemption"* (Ephesians 4:30).

When we reject God's leading time and time again, He is left with only one option. He lets us live our life absent from His power and allows us to exist in our own strength. This only leads to heartache and shame.

PUTTING IT INTO PRACTICE

Remember two truths: the only thing you can do for God is to do what He asks of you—nothing else matters. Second, He will not ask you to do anything He will not also empower you to complete.

Are you lacking strength? Is it because you are fighting for your rights? Is it because you have lost sight of the joy found in serving? Is it because you have relied on your own abilities? As you wake up each morning, remind yourself that you are the Lord's servant and ask Him for the stamina to be an excellent servant through-out the day.

Christ is your strength.

POINTS TO PONDER

- Are there areas of your life or a situation in which you are not relying on the strength of Christ? What are they?
- Recall a time when you were sure of being completely in God's strength and fully aware of it. How did this grow your faith in God or change you in others ways?
- What usually motivates you to do good work?

~ 10 ~
FREEDOM AND PEACE

*So there is now no condemnation for those who
belong to Christ Jesus. And because you belong to him,
the power of the life-giving Spirit has freed you from the power
of sin that leads to death...So letting your sinful nature control
your mind leads to death. But letting the Spirit control
your mind leads to life and peace.*
— ROMANS 8:1-2, 6-7

In the previous lesson, I shared the story of what happened when I saw a white van cross the dividing line of the freeway and smash into us. Heaven or Hell was just a fleeting moment away. What can a twenty year old man accomplish for God that would outweigh his sinful thoughts and behaviors? I went to church and Sunday school my whole life, knew the Bible pretty well and I believed it with little doubt. I honored and obeyed my parents most of the time. I tried to help people when I could, and even shared my faith with friends from time-to-time.

My accomplishments were well documented. Unknown to most were my failures. What would I do with the times I cheated in school? What about that day I stole an audio tape from the store? What about my lustful thoughts and behaviors? What about the lies? What about the poor treatment I dished out to a little brother and sister?

To the experienced sinner, my rap sheet may not seem very serious, yet to me it meant one thing—death. My spirit knew these sins were opposed to God. They were not part of His nature and He would have no fellowship with such dark things. My rap sheet was my death sentence.

It was one thing to believe God forgave me for the sins I confessed to Him, yet quite another to believe I would not receive some punishment in the next life. After-all, I deserved it. I fully understand that feelings can be deceptive—as many times as they can be accurate. So I have learned to display a stoic and calm front when emotions try to steal the more rational part of my mind. My personality tests, however, reveal that I am one of those people who teeters back and forth between a "thinker" and a "feeler."

Sometimes when my feelings engage the rational side of my mind, I learn at a deeper level. As an example, I truly believe during that brief moment facing what I thought to be certain death, I was entering into eternity free from condemnation. I can still experience the intensity of the peace which washed over me that evening when I reflect back to the still but breathing memory on highway 395. I admit this to you for a reason. I believe the greater the mortal threat, the more that peace and freedom is available through Christ.

HOW CAN WE EXPERIENCE THE FREEDOM AND PEACE OF CHRIST?

God is at peace.

Your Heavenly Father always has been at peace, and desires for you to have the same. He accomplishes this best by removing condemnation and guilt, freeing us from the feelings of shame and the ultimate punishment for sin. He offers this to those who have asked God to credit the sacrificial life, death and resurrection of Christ to their spiritual account.

This work of God through Christ is called justification. It does not change the fact sinners are guilty of sin, but it changes everything else. Practically speaking, it means that the work of Christ and one's faith in Him satisfies divine justice. Paul explains: *"And the result of God's gracious gift is very different from the result of that one man's sin. For Adam's sin led to condemnation, but God's free gift leads to our being made right with God, even though we are guilty of many sins. For the sin of this one man, Adam, caused death to rule over many. But even greater is God's wonderful grace and his gift of righteousness, for all who receive it will live in triumph over sin and death through this one man, Jesus Christ. Yes, Adam's one sin brings condemnation for everyone, but Christ's one act of righteousness brings a right relationship with God and new life for everyone. Because one person disobeyed God, many became sinners. But because one other person obeyed God, many will be made righteous"* (Romans 5:16-19).

Avoid the serious mistake of underestimating the blessings available in this life from the person and work of Jesus Christ. To do so is to miss out on the liberty He offers. Don't make the error of rejecting God's only offer which satisfies the debt of sin, His Son, Jesus Christ.

God provides freedom.

He offers the liberty of saying "no" to sin. Before you were given the gift of faith in Christ you were a slave to this world and its iniquity. You had no ability to choose, and simply did what came naturally, what felt good to your fleshly human appetite. However, as a believer, you have the ability to choose what is right because the Spirit of God enlightens and empowers you.

Freedom in Christ is designed for redemptive purposes; it is not given for self-indulgence. Our spiritual liberty gives us the ability to offer back to God what He gave to us, our lives—which He did by giving us His Son. Now we can give ourselves back to Him on a daily basis. We can say "no" to what is destructive and say "yes" to what God would have us do. Before Christ, we had no say at all. We were merely wandering around in the dark looking for the purpose of life.

God provides divine insight.

Divine thinking can set you free from the memories that haunt you, the grudges which bind you, and the insecurities that rob you. Your past, whether good or bad, can be purified into a spring of knowledge that overflows into help and wisdom for yourself and others. Your grudges can be forgiven, setting you free to experience an uninhibited compassion for all humanity. Your insecurities can be transformed into confidence.

On the other hand, your freedom to choose can be used to continue in sin, to dwell on your past, continue to hold grudges and nurture your insecurities. You can keep on doing whatever you want, even if it hurts others around you. If you do continue in these things, however, you frustrate the grace of God and distort your freedom to do good by making it a weapon of disregard to others. Paul makes this clear in 1 Corinthians 10:23-24: *"You say, 'I am allowed to do anything'—but not everything is good for you. You say, 'I am allowed to do anything'—but not everything is beneficial. Don't be concerned for your own good but for the good of others."*

Since freedom has been granted to us as undeserving people, our response should be gratefulness. Our attitude should be responsive to the desires God has for our freedom.

PUTTING IT INTO PRACTICE

Use your freedom in Christ to rid yourself of the emotional baggage of your past. If you have locked some of this in a secret hiding place within your soul known only to you and God, ask the Lord what He wants you to do with it. Maybe He will lead you to a friend, a pastor or a counselor who can provide some direction. The outcome will be the rebuilding of your personhood in Christ —it is a healing process.

Use the peace of God and the justifying work of Christ to free yourself of personal condemnation and guilt over the sins of your past. Once and for all, confess these sins to Christ and to those you have offended. Ask for forgiveness out of the sincerity of your heart. Walk away from these sins and do not allow them to taunt you ever again. If you hear their voices, remember they only intend to hurt you and mock the Jesus who died to remove them from your life.

POINTS TO PONDER

- Explain how the greater the threat to us as Christ followers— the greater peace and freedom become available through Christ.
- Do you own the freedom of redemption that Christ offers? How do you still struggle with this?

- How can you use your life experiences to help others and help yourself? How does this glorify God?
- Have you experienced the inner peace which comes from forgiving someone? Give an example.
- Have you ever felt justified in retaliation for someone else's wrong? If so, how would you handle the situation today?

~ 11 ~
YOUR SOURCE OF WISDOM

*...to those called by God to salvation, both Jews
and Gentiles, Christ is the power of God and the
wisdom of God. This foolish plan of God is wiser than
the wisest of human plans, and God's weakness is
stronger than the greatest of human strength.*
– 1 CORINTHIANS 1:24-25

"**S**ometimes you just gotta make things happen."

I have heard this phrase many times and in various venues such as sports, business, relationships, personal goals, and the list goes on. Well, that's exactly what I did. In the late 1980s, the housing market in southern California was climbing through the roof. We were renting at the time and people were yelling, "Jump in and buy now before it's too late!"

We had just started a new ministry and had very limited financial resources but we "just made it happen." In 1990 we arranged some creative financing and purchased a home without any money out of our pocket. The very next day it seemed, the housing bubble burst, at least that's how I remember it. Three years later we sold the property to move to our next ministry adventure—and lost a bundle on the transaction. I felt quite foolish because all of my financial know-how added up to a monetary loss because I lacked godly wisdom.

Before you conclude I am being too hard on myself for my lack of divine economic foresight, remember this: it is almost always true that when you force something to happen, the resistance you're pushing against may very well be the protective hand of God. That's exactly what I did; I forced the Father's hand to give me a lesson in wisdom.

"What should I do?" "I'm looking for a change." "Where should I go?" "I don't like this anymore." "How can I get this done?" "Should I or shouldn't I?" These are questions and statements I hear often and have personally said—or at least thought myself.

Our mistakes are caused first by a lack of wisdom—God's wisdom. Sometimes we say, "She needs more experience," or "He needs to slow down and think about this." Both of these statements reveal that the person in question may lack wisdom. How do we avoid such mistakes and how do we grow in understanding?

HOW DO WE OBTAIN WISDOM?

Christ is wisdom.

God's Son gives understanding to all who seek Him. The most practical and relevant piece of information for any human alive today is the Gospel of Jesus Christ. In fact, it is the *beginning* of wisdom, and the kind which grows.

Knowing Christ as Savior is the entry point into a life-long journey of learning. It is not possible for any created being to attain all the knowledge of God but the beginning is clearly marked. For example, the Old Testament book of Proverbs is an ancient collection of wise teachings that were written to impart wisdom. One of the most popular reminds us where it begins: *"Fear of the Lord is the foundation of wisdom. Knowledge of the Holy One results in good judgment"* (Proverbs 9:10).

The proverb itself is a gift which gives us the exact address to the home of wisdom. It is found in the Father's house. To dwell in the sanctuary of God is to revere and honor Him, and to learn more about Him through Jesus Christ.

Christ imparts wisdom in a variety of ways.

The Lord provides wisdom through good and bad experiences, education, observation, people, time, Scripture, and supernatural impressions. Wisdom, in general, is a relational by-product of fellowship with Christ. And a life-time of this communion will yield tremendous amounts of contentment and insight. This is the main point of attaining wisdom—to know Christ.

We often believe being wise is associated with age and time. Some boast of their vast number of years experience in one profession or another. As one man said, "I've been around the barn more times than I can remember."

When I hear that statement I often throw out a silent question in my mind, "Is it the same barn?" Because if it is I don't think I would call it wisdom. While it is generally true that understanding and common sense increases with age and time, it is dangerous to assume. If you know enough people, you are acquainted with both the wise and the foolish. This is also true of those who are well along in their years or who have plenty of experience in one area or another. One should never equate physical survival with spiritual wisdom.

God provides increased measures of understanding to those who specifically ask for it. James writes: *"If you need wisdom, ask our generous God, and he will give it to you. He will not rebuke you for asking. But when you ask him, be sure that your faith is in God alone. Do not waver, for a person with divided loyalty is as unsettled as a wave of the sea that is blown and tossed by the wind. Such people should not expect to receive anything from the Lord. Their loyalty is divided between God and the world, and they are unstable in everything they do"* (James 1:5-8).

Notice two things about these verses: God is glad to provide you wisdom, and once you ask, you should expect to receive. Actually, the meaning is even stronger. It could say, "If you don't expect to receive it, it will be sent, yet you won't experience it because you used your own methods."

So when you encounter trials, problems or a brand new challenge that seems too big, ask God for help—specifically for wisdom.

God provides even greater wisdom for those who make His will and work their central concern.

Proverbs teaches: *"Trust in the Lord with all your heart; do not depend on your own understanding. Seek his will in all you do, and he will show you which path to take. Don't be impressed with your own wisdom. Instead, fear the Lord and turn away from evil. Then you will have healing for your body and strength for your bones. Honor the Lord with your wealth and with the best part of everything you produce. Then he will fill your barns with grain, and your vats will overflow with good wine. My child, don't reject the Lord's discipline, and don't be upset when he corrects you. For the Lord corrects those he loves, just as a father corrects a child in whom he delights. Joyful is the person who finds wisdom, the one who gains understanding. For wisdom is more profitable than silver, and her wages are better than gold. Wisdom is more precious than rubies; nothing you desire can compare with her"* (Proverbs 3:5-15).

Notice the four road signs on the path to greater wisdom: Trust in God, Seek His Way, Honor the Lord with Your Wealth, Receive His Discipline. If you do these things in abundance, you will harvest wisdom.

PUTTING IT INTO PRACTICE

Ask God for His understanding and earnestly seek it in all you do. I purchased a house without diligently seeking God's wisdom. Of course I prayed, but I did not expect a clear answer; instead, I asked God to bless my own methods. I moved too soon. I'm sure the wisdom was sent but there was no such person at the address to which it was directed.

What situation are you currently experiencing where you need the wisdom of God? Take the time to ask the Lord for His thoughts and resist the temptation to act before hearing from Him. You may hear from heaven through godly counsel or you may receive a strong impression from the Lord. Be sure not to make a decision before you hear!

POINTS TO PONDER

- Can you recall ever "forcing the hand of God?" When you took matters into your own hands– what happened? What did you learn from the experience? How do you think things would have turned out if you hadn't rushed the situation?

- What changes can you make in your life so that this doesn't happen again? How can you start to seek God's wisdom in all you do?
- Have you ever met an individual you thought was very wise? What made them seem this way?
- What are the various ways that God imparts wisdom to you?

~ 12 ~

THE HEART OF CHRIST

Then Jesus said, "Come to me, all of you
who are weary and carry heavy burdens, and I
will give you rest. Take my yoke upon you. Let me
teach you, because I am humble and gentle at heart,
and you will find rest for your souls. For my yoke is
easy to bear, and the burden I give you is light."
– MATTHEW 11:28-30

Greatness is a subject found in the Bible. It is often defined as a pinnacle of achievement in a specific field of endeavor. Most of us think of greatness as being the very best at something. Unfortunately, this definition of success leaves out most of us because there can only be one "greatest" of anything.

The Bible teaches us about God's definition of accomplishment at the highest level of life. He has given all of us gifts and allows the circumstances of our lives to frame the context of our abilities and opportunities. In other words, He knows our limitations and our possibilities. His desire is quite simple. He wants us to offer ourselves in the best ways and for the most important purposes possible within the boundaries He has established.

As a young Christian I found myself trying to be just like the people I admired. I tried to preach or teach like so and so. I even tried to look like certain people and do what they did. I found myself using their vocabulary and the same philosophies of life. This is normal for young people experimenting with their personhood. And it is good to notice the positive qualities in others and try to integrate them. But if we are not careful, we will live a life that misses the point of our human experience.

God didn't make you to be like anyone else but the Christ within you. To be like Christ is to mirror Him in character—and to be like you is to be true to your uniqueness in calling and giftedness. This is why Jesus calls those who are weary to come to Him and find rest, because He provides a labor that fits the possibilities He designed for you.

It just doesn't make sense to transform you into someone else, rather the person God intended. Let's face it. You will never become that other individual, and just the *trying* consumes too much energy. But you can become like Christ in character because He lives within your heart. You can also discover and develop your uniqueness because of the helping presence of the Holy Spirit.

Remember, there is only *one* of each person God has created. He does not make duplicates. Your greatness is determined by how well you become the person God formed you to be within the context He gave you to live within. The Lord does not expect more than this; He simply expects the truth.

WHAT IS THE HEART OF CHRIST?

The heart of Christ is difficult to miss.

Perhaps the most quoted verse in the Bible is found in John 3:16, but the verse that follows is less remembered, yet constructs the context of the prior. Let's revisit: *"For God loved the world so much that he gave his one and only Son, so that everyone who believes in him will not perish but have eternal life. God sent his son into the world not to judge the world, but to save the world through him"* (John 3:16-17).

These verses are of utmost importance to understand the heart of God. There are two things in the human experience that are held in tension with one another: the heart of God and the will of humanity. The heart of God is clear; He is a giver, not a taker. Sadly, the majority of people reject His heart.

Jesus said most people travel a wide road which leads to destruction and few find the narrow road which leads to life. Obviously, Jesus knows the truth and we must embrace the sober fact most people take the wrong path. Nevertheless, the narrow road—the heart of God—is difficult to miss because of the many off-ramps He provides. The main road is wide; however, all along this wide slab of destruction are off-ramps which lead to the Road of Life.

The heart of Christ is patient.

The Gospel writer John describes the patience of Christ's heart when he recorded Peter's encounter with Jesus after the resurrection. Peter was a spirited soul who often made courageous and sometime prideful remarks and gestures. But in the end he really blew it. When Jesus needed his affection the most, Peter turned his back on Him. Jesus was crucified and Peter experienced shame.

After the resurrection, Jesus found Peter doing his old things. He went back to what he knew he could do, making a living at fishing. He no longer saw himself as a warrior, a hero, and certainly not a man of God. Peter probably considered Jesus a friend, but was ashamed of being the far lesser of the two. And he was certain the resurrected Jesus would no longer trust him with any more responsibilities.

As you probably know, Jesus first restored Peter by reconciling their relationship. Then He sealed the bond by challenging him to pick up where he left off prior to his cowardice and sin. Not long after, Peter preached a message where 3,000 present became believers and were baptized. This man made more mistakes in his life, yet the Lord used him. One of his gifts was obviously the gift of preaching, and the Lord blessed his efforts even though he was once a traitor and a failure.

The heart of Christ desires partnership.

Jesus said, "Take my yoke upon you." A yoke was a rabbi's teaching.

It was what he required from his disciples. Jesus described His yoke as *"easy"* (Matthew 11:28-30). His heart is relational. He does not desire to give you or me a yoke to bear alone. He wants to bear it with us—together.

The work the Lord desires for us is a good work. It is a plowing that not only makes a difference in the world, it also benefits us. By sharing part of the labor and seeing the success of God in the world, we gain a sense of ownership.

Participating in good work is one of the blessings of life. Unfortunately, many of us go about our work alone. We plow along without realizing the Spirit of Christ is longing to share the labor with us. When we leave Christ out of our daily activities, we live an existence which leads to feeble results lacking the presence of God's joy and power.

PUTTING IT INTO PRACTICE

Always, regardless of the situation, run into the arms of Christ. No matter what you have done, never, never run away. Allow God to define you and grow you into the person He intended. Now is the time to get alone with God and meditate on the things you know to be true about how the Creator designed you.

Set some time aside and begin to write down the things you know are true about you. Describe how you came to the narrow road. Record what you feel in your heart. Do you dream big dreams or do you secretly plan small acts of kindness for those around you. Remember to not compare yourself to others. Ask God what is true about *you*. What is in you that is from Him? Then ask the Father to develop these in you as they are in Christ.

POINTS TO PONDER

- Why is it a "fruitless mission" to try and be like someone else. Why is it against God's will to do so?

67

- What are the differences between traveling the wide road and the narrow road?
- What do you truly like about yourself? What would you change if you could?
- When are you most weary? Do you have anyone who would share the burden? How would you like them to help?

ESSENTIAL NUMBER TWO

FOLLOWING CHRIST

As we improve our knowledge of Christ, we grow in our trust and are more willing to follow Him.

Sadly, some never move closer to the Lord because they feel safe keeping the same distance they have kept for years. If your desire is to *decrease* the space between you and Christ, what you are about to discover will help you reach this objective.

Let me warn, however, that the following subjects do not follow the form of any one Christian denomination. My goal here has nothing to do with supporting the claims of a particular Christian group.

At this point in life I have learned two things to be true about the church: First, God loves every local congregation within the global church, and the local body of believers is the vehicle the Lord uses to express His love for us. His ultimate mission is to change the world through His people, not the institution. Second, the church is too often wrong and at times too full of itself.

My goal is to express my love for Christ, His church, you, and those who have not yet believed upon Jesus. This is why I want to get you off to a good start as His follower.

My teaching will always lead you to and through the local church because this is how Jesus set things up. However, I will never place your involvement in a local congregation over your commitment to follow the Lord—the way He is *worthy* of being. In short, get involved in a church that is serious about following Jesus.

~ 13 ~
FOLLOW

*Then Jesus said to his disciples, "If any of you wants
to be my follower, you must turn from your selfish ways, take up
your cross, and follow me. If you try to hang on to your life, you
will lose it. But if you give up your life for my sake, you will save
it. And what do you benefit if you gain the whole world but lose
your own soul? Is anything worth more than your soul?"*
— MATTHEW 16:24-26

We have all met them. They are alive and well and living among us—and some we are willing to call our friends. I am speaking of those who live within our communities, but are not really part of community.

There is a spirit of independence so fierce it is sometimes unknown even to the person infected. These self-sufficient souls are not the hermits who live alone on a deserted island, they *are* the island. Such a person feels no need to belong to a fellowship unless it is willing to move to the island and abide by the rules established. You will never know this "island soul" because he or she participates only in what is required and never stays in one community long enough to become a vital member.

The island soul is wounded, and in the interest of self-preservation, has created a lifestyle free from the imperfections of human organizations and relationships which can cause pain. They may work in your office, go to your school, or even attend your church but they rarely adhere to the values of the community. They simply do *what* they want, *when* they want.

To be a disciple of Jesus Christ is to walk into the crowds of people, not away from them. This is called ministry and it is the way of Christ. In biblical terms, to minister is to serve, and serving in the name of Jesus is a privilege and a high calling.

Many do not experience this joy because they are preoccupied with their own affairs. Others avoid serving because they are not willing to follow Christ with their wounds exposed. However, Jesus has called you as a believer to follow *regardless* of your life situation. In the process you will always receive more than you can possibly give.

THREE WAYS TO FOLLOW CHRIST:

First: To follow Jesus is to follow Him <u>publicly</u>.

Jesus describes this idea in mission terminology. We are called to lay aside personal agendas, pick up His cause in our lives and share it with the world. This is why God's Son says, *"If any of you wants to be my follower, you must turn from your selfish ways, take up your cross, and follow me"* (Matthew 16:24).

Ambition is not evil when it is selfless. It only becomes dangerous when it is attached to temporary concerns, which dwell within the boundary of time and reflect a philosophy of success foreign to heaven. These concerns include such aspirations as fame, fortune, pride, and power. Eternal matters transcend time and space—just like God. This kind of living is likened to a valued warrior. Paul writes, *"Endure suffering along with me, as a good soldier of Christ Jesus. Soldiers don't get tied up in the affairs of civilian life, for then they cannot please the officer who enlisted them"* (2 Timothy 2:3-4).

Jesus uses the metaphor of shouldering or carrying a cross to describe the public nature of His mission. The cross reminds people of crucifixion, which in the day of Christ was a public event. It was designed to punish criminals and insurgents in such a way that all could see the pain and shame. It served as an effective warning and deterrent to all who witnessed it.

The point Jesus is making is clear. To follow Him will require a public commitment and may involve severe testing which at times may be visible to others. But don't rush to the garage and build yourself a wooden cross. Instead, to pick up one's cross is to live unashamed of

Christ, undeterred by the tests and threats which will surely come.

Second: Your public journey begins with public baptism.

Jesus' ministry began immediately following His baptism by John in the Jordan River. Though Jesus had no sin to confess, He humbled Himself to illustrate the importance of submission to the Father. John felt ridiculous baptizing the Son of God, so he objected. This is how Jesus responded: *"'It should be done, for we must carry out all that God requires.' So John agreed to baptize him"* (Matthew 3:15).

Let's look at this another way. God vows to redeem souls who trust in the person and ministry of Jesus for their forgiveness and resurrection. It is only reasonable to accept such a vow by expressing thanks to God through baptism. In a sense, this is how Jesus' public ministry is visually introduced to each new believer. Baptism is a public symbol of Jesus' death, burial, and resurrection.

Paul explains this symbolism: *"For you were buried with Christ when you were baptized. And with him you were raised to a new life because you trusted the mighty power of God, who raised Christ from the dead"* (Colossians 2:12).

When you are laid back under the water, it is a picture of you dying to your own agenda. Then, as you are raised up out of the water, it is an image of coming to life with God's agenda. You are dying to self and being raised to live for Christ. Through this physical act, we see the forgiveness of sin and the resurrection of Jesus Christ, as well as our future bodily resurrection.

Water baptism is your first opportunity to "pick up your cross" publicly. It does not make you a Christian; it is what Christians do to honor Christ. It is like a wedding ring. The ring does not make you married, but it is a symbol of your commitment to your spouse.

Don't let others tell you water baptism is not important. Jesus commanded it and He has not changed His mind. This public expression with water is a joyous occasion to share one's faith in Christ. As believing and unbelieving friends and family members witness baptism, they are being introduced or reminded of the person and ministry of Jesus. In this way, His message is told over and over again.

Third: Your journey is to be shared within <u>community</u>.

Christ has called believers to be in fellowship with other Christians—to be an attached member of the Body. God compares the Body of believers to the human body. Arms, toes, and fingers were all designed to be attached to the body, and a Christ follower lives this out by connecting to a local fellowship.

Notice again the teaching on community: *"If you try to hang on to your life, you will lose it. But if you give up your life for my sake, you will save it. And what do you benefit if you gain the whole world but lose your own soul? Is anything worth more than your soul?"* (Matthew 16:25-26).

The key phrase here is "If you try to hang on to your life..." Instead, we are called to give ourselves to God by becoming a participating member of His Body. We do this by committing to His cause and inviting those who are unattached to join the community of Christ.

Along with baptism, followers gather around what is called the "Lord's Table." Some know it as *communion* and some the *Eucharist.* It is a time when Christians gather to remember two important things: the literal and sacrificial act of Jesus Christ and the Lord's call for unity within the spiritual Body of Christ. Paul explains: *"For I pass on to you what I received from the Lord himself. On the night when he was betrayed, the Lord Jesus took some bread and gave thanks to God for it. Then he broke it in pieces and said, 'This is my body, which is given for you. Do this to remember me.' In the same way, he took the cup of wine after supper, saying, 'This cup is the new covenant between God and his people—an agreement confirmed with my blood. Do this to remember me as often as you drink it.' For every time you eat this bread and drink this cup, you are announcing the Lord's death until he comes again"* (1 Corinthians 11:23-26).

Jesus created these symbols to help us remember Him and the importance of uniting with others around Him and His mission. Together, Jesus and the disciples ate the bread and drank from the cup, representing His body and blood given for us. For all Christ has done for you and me, the very least we can do is to honor Him by making our faith public and uniting with His Body.

PUTTING IT INTO PRACTICE

If you have not been baptized, now is the time. The mysterious initiation of baptism expresses a love received and returned. Speak with a pastor this week and start your public mission as a follower of Jesus.

Also, if you have not joined a local church, make this a high priority. Look for a congregation that is centered on Christ's mission. Stay away from groups which are self-serving and inward-focused.

If you have been baptized as a believer and are part of a church, commit yourself to encouraging and assisting others in this process of discovery and obedience. This is where "following" begins.

POINTS TO PONDER

- Describe a person who has either led you to Christ or was a strong example of following Jesus.
- How does God use His people to impact others? How do you believe He can also use you?
- What does baptism and communion mean to you personally?

~ 14 ~
READ GOD'S WORD

I have hidden your word in my heart,
that I might not sin against you.
— PSALM 119:11

W hen I was sixteen, my father told me to be sure to regularly check the oil level in the engine of my car. He explained how engines burn oil and without it, the motor would burn up. Did I listen? Apparently not! One summer evening while driving home, my car began to smoke and ran completely out of power following a loud clanking noise. As I sat on the side of a mountain road, I could hear the replay of my father's warning.

I cannot recall the number of times I have been lost on the roads of California or other states. The confidence I placed in my "good sense of direction" has failed me time and time again. Sometimes the result of my self-reliance was more damaging than simply asking for directions at the corner store. I have arrived late to important meetings and received a speeding ticket while trying to make up for the time I spent being lost. The possibilities could be much worse, but those I have experienced were inexcusable and did not reflect the image of Christ within me.

Often I have tried to assemble a product without reading the instructions. This is embarrassing, but true. One would think I would learn from my mistakes, considering that I often fail to assemble the item properly!

I didn't listen to my father's advice concerning the oil because I was immature. I didn't look at road maps because I was self-reliant. I didn't read the instructions because I was impatient.

If the truth were told, many of us have attempted to follow Jesus without the advice of those wiser, without following a spiritual road map, and without reading the owner's manual. The Holy Bible is all of these. The B-I-B-L-E is our Basic Instructions Before Leaving Earth.

WHY SCRIPTURE IS IMPORTANT

To follow Jesus is to <u>trust</u> Scripture.

The Bible consists of 66 different books, written over a period of 1,600 years (approximately 1,500 BC to AD 100). The Spirit of God directed the thoughts of more than 40 kings, prophets, leaders and followers of Jesus.

The books of the Bible were collected, arranged and recognized as inspired and sacred writings throughout time by councils of rabbis and church leaders, based upon very specific guidelines. The primary rule of authority for a book to be included in the New Testament (Books of the New Covenant) was that it had to be written by an apostle or someone close to an apostle. This standard ensured the eyewitness accounts of Jesus and the foundational years of the church.

The most significant discovery in recent times that affirms our trust in the Old Testament is what we now call the Dead Sea Scrolls. In 1947, a young shepherd lost one of his animals on the slopes at the northwest end of the Dead Sea. As he wandered into a cave, he found large jars containing leather scrolls which had gone undetected for over 1,800 years. These scrolls were the library of a religious group that settled about eight miles south of Jericho over 100 years before the birth of Jesus.

Several additional caves were found as a result of the first accidental discovery. These contained many different rooms: a Scriptorium (where scribes copied the Scriptures), a potter's workshop (where they made the jars to keep the manuscripts cool and safe from contaminating elements), a kitchen, a bakery, baptism cisterns, and a cemetery. The Jewish War of A.D. 66-73 caused the site to be abandoned.

Within these caves nearly 100 fragments of the Old Testament books of Exodus, Leviticus, Numbers, Deuteronomy, Jeremiah, Job, Psalms and Ruth were found. Fragments were discovered from all the Old

Testament books except for Esther. These discoveries reflect amazing accuracy to the texts we read from today.

Throughout time, God has been faithful to continue His self-revelation and to preserve these for every generation. The prophet Isaiah echoes this fact: *"The grass withers and the flowers fade, but the word of our God stands forever"* (Isaiah 40:8).

To follow Jesus is to <u>ingest</u> Scripture.

Changing the way a person thinks changes how a person lives, relates to others and to God. The Scriptures instill a worldview from heaven's perspective, bringing all of life into an understandable context.

Truth has greater power than fantasy because in the end, reality simply *reflects* truth. Jesus often demonstrated His understanding of truth through His personal knowledge of the Old Testament. In the following example, Jesus knew that God would reveal His Son to the world in spite of the Jews rejection. To the priests and elders in Jerusalem, He asked, *"Didn't you ever read this in the Scriptures? The stone that the builders rejected has now become the cornerstone. This is the Lord's doing, and it is wonderful to see. I tell you, the Kingdom of God will be taken away from you and given to a nation that will produce the proper fruit"* (Matthew 21:42-43).

Jesus is quoting verses from the 118th Psalm. In so doing, He illustrates that truth can be accepted or rejected, but neither decision can change it. Instead our choices concerning truth affect our eternal destiny and life experience.

The New Testament joins the Old Testament in declaring the wisdom of God's Word. Hebrews 4:12 describes the spiritual surgery Scripture can affect: *"For the word of God is alive and powerful. It is sharper than the sharpest two-edged sword, cutting between soul and spirit, between joint and marrow. It exposes our innermost thoughts and desires."*

Paul sheds more light on the energy of Scripture: *"All Scripture is inspired by God and is useful to teach us what is true and to make us realize what is wrong in our lives. It corrects us when we are wrong and teaches us to do what is right. God uses it to prepare and equip his people to do every good work"* (2 Timothy 3:16-17).

Here is the two-step process of following Jesus through Scripture: First, we come to know our true selves as Hebrews 4 describes. Second, it gives us new and positive direction so we can discover how God wants us to live. Spirituality is just as practical as it is mysterious. The Lord is preparing us to do "every good work" He desires.

PUTTING IT INTO PRACTICE

Read God's Word every day. Perhaps you will use one of the excellent Bible reading programs available. Don't just read; write down what you learn until it becomes like listening to God.

Ask yourself, "What internal step can I take which demonstrates I am imitating Jesus?" For example, say: "Today I choose to cultivate a spirit that listens to others the way Jesus did."

What actions will you take which reflect the new person developing inside? For example: "I will ask John how he feels about his current conflict with his father and I will sincerely listen with my face, body, heart and ears."

POINTS TO PONDER

- How has reading the Bible changed your life?
- Quote one or two Scriptures which have made a personal impact on you.
- What commitment will you make concerning the study of Scripture?

~ 15 ~
Be Ready

Teach those who are rich in this world not to be proud and not to trust in their money, which is so unreliable. Their trust should be in God, who richly gives us all we need for our enjoyment. Tell them to use their money to do good. They should be rich in good works and generous to those in need, always being ready to share with others. By doing this they will be storing up their treasure as a good foundation for the future so that they may experience true life.
– 1 Timothy 6:17-19

I don't remember the name of the movie or the story line, but I do remember the ending. The lead actor was so distraught by the events of his life that he decided to commit suicide. His chosen method was to swim out into the ocean as far as he could until finally he drowns from exhaustion.

As he is paddling in the sea, he is speaking to himself all the reasons why he is going to take his own life. In his view, much of the reasoning has to do with the way God allowed his journey to evolve the way it had. The more he vented, the further he swam—until the moment of truth arrived. Exhausted and within seconds of going under to his death, he had a change of heart.

This man then began to ask God for forgiveness, admitting that most of the events in his life were his own doing. As he turned and headed for shore, let me paraphrase what he said: "God, if you get me out of this mess I will serve You the rest of my life and give You 100% of my income and possessions."

As his strength increased, so did his hope for survival. A few minutes later he promised, "God, if you get me out of this mess, I will give you 90%...." The closer he came to the shore the less he offered the Lord. Finally when he arrived on the sand, he exclaimed, "God, what am I talking about? You're the One who got me in this mess in the first place!"

The scene was designed to be humorous and it was, because it had a ring of truth. It reminds us how unprepared we are to really live a life for God, full of assignments, challenges, and surprises.

THREE REALITIES:

One: To follow Jesus, we must be ready to accept whatever circumstances come our way.

Some of us are born into poverty, others to wealth, and most remain in the middle. Some have been blessed with good health, while others suffer from ailments and diseases. There are people who come from good families, still others are trying to recover from a history of relational pain. Some of us have seen many of our dreams come true, while others are wondering what went wrong. Many have been relatively free from the experience of a painful divorce or an untimely death in our families, but others have had more than their fair share.

To follow Jesus is to follow Him regardless of circumstances. As strange as it seems, those moments in our lives that are the most peaceful can be the times we drift from the path of Christ. Notice Paul's words to those who appear to be self-sufficient in their wealth: *"Teach those who are rich in this world not to be proud and not to trust in their money, which is so unreliable. Their trust should be in God, who richly gives us all we need for our enjoyment"* (1 Timothy 6:17).

Two feelings can surface from good times: pride and guilt. Pride is belief in the lie within us that we somehow deserve the good things we have. Perhaps we say, "I have this or that because I have worked hard." We might also think, "I have done things right." While both of these statements may contain some truth, they are lacking full knowledge, which reminds us God has endowed us with the ability to work and has given us the wisdom we needed. Our fellow disciple, James, speaks of this truth: *"Whatever is good and perfect comes down to us from God..."* (James 1:17).

Then there are those who feel guilty for being blessed with health, riches, and other delightful circumstances. These feelings do not come from heaven. We should trade in this sense of guilt for the attitude of humility. When we are humble, even though we may be rich, we no longer trust in fate, but in God. New Christians tend to trust in circumstances; maturing believers *evaluate* the circumstances and their possibilities. Both positive and difficult situations can be used for our good.

Two: To follow Jesus, we must be ready to direct our <u>resources</u> toward His purposes.

Unfortunately, many use their gifts, education, possessions and experience to nurture self-serving interests without generously sharing with people in need. Those who are guilty of living this kind of life-style simply have not been challenged to focus their lives in such a way as to become an instrument of God's grace. This transformation is based upon a major change in thinking. Instead of becoming a reservoir, storing up personal pleasures, one becomes a funnel God uses to bless others. When this lifestyle is developed, the resources of heaven continue to flow because God can trust such a person.

For those who claim to follow Jesus, this idea is not an option. We are to examine the inventory of our lives and be stewards as God directs us. As Paul writes: *"Tell them to use their money to do good. They should be rich in good works and generous to those in need, always being ready to share with others"* (1 Timothy 6:18).

The local church is God's storehouse of resources. It is here we find people, experience, talent, money, and Christ's mission to transform lives. As we generously support the local church, we see abundant ministry flow into the lives of those within the congregation, community, and around the world. One of the key reasons the local church can be a distribution center of God's blessings is because Christians do not buy everything they can afford. Their focus is on the mission of Jesus Christ.

The mission-minded local church designs ministries to meet needs through the sharing of the Gospel, feeding the poor, training believers and sending out missionaries into the marketplace, schools, hospices and around the globe.

God challenges every follower of Christ to make giving a high priority. The prophet Malachi shares these startling words from Heaven sent to the people of God: *"'You have cheated me of the tithes and offerings due to me. You are under a curse, for your whole nation has been cheating me. Bring all the tithes into the storehouse so there will be enough food in my Temple. If you do,' says the Lord of Heaven's Armies, 'I will open the windows of heaven for you. I will pour out a blessing so great you won't have enough room to take it in! Try it! Put me to the test! Your crops will be abundant, for I will guard them from insects and disease. Your grapes will not fall from the vine before they are ripe,' says the Lord of Heaven's Armies. Then all nations will call you blessed, for your land will be such a delight'"* (Malachi 3:8-12).

For followers of Christ, this attitude is not a burden or a religious drudgery. It is what we do joyfully because of the eternal riches we have in Christ. We have no need God will not provide and no future we should worry over. We are in the business of allowing Heaven to invade earth.

Three: To follow Jesus, we must be ready to live a life of adventure.

Following God's Son is not a cycle of boring rituals or religious duties, rather a mission that values vision over security. Plus, it is what the apostle Paul describes as "real life." We cannot experience such an existence unless we are ready to be who He wants us to be, go where He wants us to go, and do what He wants us to do. Larry Crabb in *Shattered Dreams* shares a similar idea: "Faith, as I am growing to understand it more, is about looking beyond my circumstances to a person. To have faith in better circumstances, even in God creating better circumstances, is not true faith. I want to be the kind of man who can watch every dream go down in flames and still yearn to be intimately involved in kingdom living, intimately involved with my friend the King, and still be willing to take another risk just because it delights Him for me to do so. And my flesh shivers to think about it."

PUTTING IT INTO PRACTICE

Ask God what He wants you to do with the resources He has given you. What changes do you need to make in your financial management, time scheduling, or in the stewardship of your gifts and talents? What experiences should be used to help others? To assist you in this process, read 2 Corinthians 9:6-15 and memorize verses 7 and 8.

POINTS TO PONDER

- What gifts do you have right now?
- What gifts do you believe God is growing in you?
- Have you ever had to deal with pride or guilt? If so, how did you overcome them?
- Recall an experience where you had to trust God regarding your financial resources. What did you learn from the experience?

~ 16 ~
BE FAITHFUL

The master was full of praise. "Well done, my good
and faithful servant. You have been faithful in handling this
small amount, so now I will give you many more
responsibilities. Let's celebrate together!"

– MATTHEW 25:21

Some good friends told me about a hummingbird nest in a bush outside their front door. Like many of us, they were quite interested in observing God's mysterious creations, and became very animated as they described this hummingbird family and its environment. The nest was smaller than the palm of a child's hand; the eggs were easy to miss, and of course the baby birds were very fragile.

As time went on they noticed something they didn't expect. While they were waiting to see how the fledglings would learn how to fly (some flap their wings 55 times per second and fly 25 mph), the nest started to disintegrate and fall apart. Their home suddenly became too delicate to sustain the ounces of weight the birds gained as they grew. To put this in perspective, a toothpick placed on a hummingbird's nest looks similar to what a large tree would look like laying on top of a child's playhouse.

From what I have heard it is unusual for all the young hummingbirds to survive. In this case however, both birds did, causing the nest to fall apart under the strain and leaving them no other choice but to fly out into a new adventure. According to my friends, these young birds did just fine.

As I began to think about this story I was reminded of what happens to people when they mature. Healthy individuals and organizations grow—this is normal. However, as they develop, they become too big for their environment. Kids grow out of their shoes and clothes and they graduate from one grade to the next. Adults, if they are faithful and diligent, advance from one job to the next and one skill to another. The hummingbird nest reminds us that healthy creatures grow into new challenges, where further development and influence can occur.

WHAT DOES FAITHFULNESS LOOK LIKE?

Faithfulness starts by recognizing what God has left in your care.

Jesus tells His disciples a story of a man who divided up his possessions among three of his servants while he went on a journey. He distributed his funds among them according to their abilities. To one he gave five talents (over $5,000), to another two, and to the other, one talent.

God continues to do this today. To each of us He has entrusted a portion of wealth (talent, experience, relationship, opportunity and finances). He typically does this based upon our family heritage, our spiritual gifts, our surroundings, our education, and many other factors. The point we must not miss is that God includes *everyone* in this process. Some receive a little and others much, yet nobody is left out. The Lord desires that we grow the resources entrusted to us, regardless of whether we have received little or much.

Faithfulness involves investing the resources He has given you for the good of the Kingdom.

Kingdom work is God's work—which can take many forms. It can be to bless a friend, help the poor, building up the local church or investing in your family. It can involve solving human problems. The key is, God wants His resources to influence the world toward the person and ministry of Jesus Christ.

The Lord continues to illustrate His story by describing the activities of these three servants. The first two servants went right to work and invested all which was placed in their care, resulting in the doubling of the original investment. The third servant was either too worried about losing the money or too lazy to do anything with it. He simply held onto the talents. When confronted, the servant called the master "a difficult man" and revealed his lack of understanding. He did not comprehend that the talent given to him was designed to produce growth.

Faithfulness results in greater influence and responsibilities.

The first two servants graduated to greater responsibilities and influence which brought much joy to their master. The third was separated from his talent and was thrown out of the master's kingdom because he was never a genuine member of the family. If he were, he would have known that the master's influence caused all his endeavors to grow. In other words, it is not the servant who produces the increase; it is the influence of the master which causes the growth. We are simply called to be faithful and invest what God has presented to us. He is the one who allows it to multiply.

PUTTING IT INTO PRACTICE

Right now, list the resources God has placed in your care. Start with people. Who is in your circle of influence? Who should you be investing your life into? Note other valuable treasures (income, talent, time, ideas, vision, opportunities, assets, etc.) which have been loaned to you by the Lord.

Once you have identified these, offer the list to God in prayer and ask Him for the wisdom to demonstrate faithfulness in multiplying His investments in you. Then begin to plan, as a Christ follower would, what you are going to do with what God has laid in your hands. Share these thoughts with those who also desire to increase God's favor and ask for their feedback and encouragement.

POINTS TO PONDER

- Of the gifts God has given you, which do you feel are the most significant?
- What part does the Lord play in the development of these gifts?
- How do you use a particular talent for the glory of God's Kingdom instead of for your own benefit?

~ 17 ~
BE TEACHABLE

*...the one who received the seed that fell
on good soil is the man who hears the word and
understands it. He produces a crop, yielding a
hundred, sixty or thirty times what was sown.*
– MATTHEW 13:23 NIV

Without a doubt, the most enjoyable people to work with are those with teachable hearts. Unfortunately, many of us have had the experience of working with individuals who just don't listen. They may look as if they are paying attention, but they are actually busy formulating their next rebuttal or excuse. When you finish talking, they immediately open their mouths and reveal they didn't hear one word you said.

The Proverbs identify such people in a terrible way calling them "fools" (Proverbs 18:2).

The very fact you are reading this book demonstrates your willingness to be teachable. You are investing your time in learning how to follow Christ, instead of the many other options available.

WHAT DOES IT LOOK LIKE TO BE TEACHABLE?

To be teachable is a matter of the heart.

The Biblical proverbs scream out this truth: *"Above all else, guard your heart, for it affects everything you do"* (Proverbs 4:23). In order to be willing to learn, we need to take care of our inner person—our heart.

Using soil as a metaphor, Jesus tells a story to illustrate what it means to guard our hearts as one of His followers. In Matthew 13:1-9, He shares how a farmer spread seed that fell on four different surfaces: (1) a road next to the farm land, (2) shallow soil due to the underlying rock, (3) soil which has not been cleared of roots, thorns and weeds, and (4) soil that has been properly tilled and prepared for planting. Other than the road, the planting surfaces look similar to the human eye. The differences between these three soils lie below the surface—let's dig them up and see!

A teachable heart is not a <u>shallow</u> heart.

The seeds which landed on the footpath were quickly eaten by hungry birds. Then, *"Other seeds fell on shallow soil with underlying rock..."* (v.5). These had little hope for bearing fruit because there was a large slab of stone just inches below the surface. Yes, you may plant and see some growth, but the soil can't sustain life. It is unable to maintain the moisture needed during the scorching heat.

This situation resembles the person whose hardness of heart lies below a surface of shallow cooperation. In tough times, this individual will not be moved to follow Christ. He or she is only interested in instant results —character is simply not important. Jesus' example of the rocky soil describes the "fair weather" friend.

Shallow people never accomplish anything of significance because they can't take the heat required in the desert of perseverance.

A teachable heart is not a <u>distracted</u> heart.

Jesus spoke of seed planted in soil which may have looked the same as other ground, but lurking beneath the surface were roots, weeds and thorns, *"...that grew up and choked out the tender plants"* (v.7). This soil presents a paradox. The crop grows, but there is great competition from other suffocating plant life.

The Lord is describing a well-meaning person who probably struggles with one of two major areas in life: *fixing* things or *gaining* things.

A person trying to fix everything—relationships, finances, asset management or life maintenance—ends up dying with everything in order, except their heart. Such an individual is usually focused on problems, worries and cares instead of purpose.

On the other hand, a person centered on *gaining* things is trying to taste every opportunity and achieve worldly success. Instead they end up missing the true meaning of life and risking their soul in the process.

We often see people attempt to accumulate worldly wealth, while trying to honor God at the same time. Can it be done? Jesus says: *"No one can serve two masters. For you will hate one and love the other; you will be devoted to one and despise the other. You cannot serve both God and money"* (Matthew 6:24).

The distracted heart is common among believers. The problem is focus—most of us are simply trying to do too much. Here's a partial list of the good things we pursue:

Vocation • Friends • Marriage • Ministry • Recreation
• Parents • Children • Education • Exercise • Responsibilities
• Church • Community • Investments • Business • Travel
• Reading • Writing • Serving • Visiting • Eating

However, none of these should master us. When they do, our heart becomes choked of its very life.

A teachable heart is not a *perfect* heart.

Jesus calls the third type of soil *"good."* (Matthew 15:23)—not "perfect." He says it can produce 30, 60, or even 100 times more than the original seed. Good soil is not completely without weeds and rocks, but it has been sufficiently cultivated so that the crop will flourish despite the threat of heat and weeds.

The Master is describing an imperfect person who listens with his or her whole heart. He is painting a picture of one who still has some weeds and a few stones, yet desires to understand and live for the purposes of God. They are not just willing to *listen* to Christ, but to *follow* Him.

Those who are teachable have hearts which are well cultivated and ready to receive instruction, purpose and wisdom:

- They are capable of foolish things, but they are not fools.
- They are capable of being shallow from time-to-time, but they are not continually shallow.
- They are capable of being distracted by the things of this world, but they soon regain their focus.

Are you teachable?

PUTTING IT INTO PRACTICE

Most careful people try to align their priorities with the things they value. Professional life-coaches often guide students through this process by helping them organize their lives. This activity is of some value; however, it lacks the central truth we can glean from this lesson: God values a heart He can teach. We need a different perspective. It's not important what we treasure; it is important what God treasures.

Instead of making a list of priorities or values, fan them out around the centrality of Christ. Notice in the diagram below how Christ is at the core. He is not listed as the first of several, rather He is the *central* priority. There's a big difference.

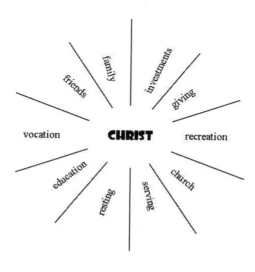

A priority ranking suggests that there comes a time when you leave one stage and move to the next, but when one factor is at the core it implies that the same priority is present in all the others.

This week contemplate what it means to make Christ the primary focus of your life. Then ask for His help to help you place all the other priorities around Him and fill each of these areas with His presence.

POINTS TO PONDER

- Looking at the above illustration, which would you rank as your top five priorities? How much of a part does Christ play in these?
- What barriers do people erect which hinders their "teachability"?
- What daily steps can you take to keep the soil of your heart prepared to receive God's seed?

~18~
BE OBEDIENT

But anyone who hears and doesn't obey is
like a person who builds a house without a foundation.
When the floods sweep down against that house,
it will collapse into a heap of ruins.

– LUKE 6:49

With tears running down her face, permit me to paraphrase what Darlene said, "Many wonderful memories are in this place: baptisms, funerals, marriages, dedications and salvations. Personally, I don't want to move, but we need to in order to make room for the people God loves and those we are called to love."

She shared these words from her seat at a pivotal point in the history of our church. The ministry was at a crossroads. After stagnating for some time, it began to grow and there was a vision to sell the property and begin the process of relocation.

This dear woman was one of a handful of patriarchs left in our congregation. She was loved and respected by all and her words were more powerful than she will ever know. Darlene could have led a campaign to preserve the days gone by out of reverence for history and tradition, but this is not what she did. Instead, she stood up among us and encouraged the congregation to move ahead. She taught us the meaning of obedience.

We thought Darlene could not contribute more than she was already doing. Her vocation was nursing and she was a beloved caregiver. In the mobile home park where she lived, she was a light of love and service to those around her. In the church she enjoyed serving the parents by providing care for the young ones. She volunteered for everything she was able to do. This is why she had influence.

Obedience to Christ is what we saw in Darlene's life everyday. But at this particular turning-point moment, she demonstrated a type of obedience which went beyond the norm—and the church moved forward.

WHY IS OBEDIENCE SO IMPORTANT?

Obedience is the foundation of active faith.

If a person claims to have faith in Christ, but does not listen and obey, he is just like a house built on the beach without any stable foundation. Once a major storm hits the structure, it will probably fall to pieces because it has no solid support beneath it. This is exactly the analogy Jesus used in Luke 6:49.

I cannot count the number of people I have called a brother or sister in Christ who later were devastated by a tempest— most often caused by their own lack of obedience. And I must readily admit that many of my own troubles have been caused by disobedience.

The apostle Paul reminds us of this same principle: *"Don't be misled—you cannot mock the justice of God. You will always harvest what you plant. Those who live only to satisfy their own sinful nature will harvest decay and death from that sinful nature. But those who live to please the Spirit will harvest everlasting life from the Spirit. So let's not get tired of doing what is good. At just the right time we will reap a harvest of blessing if we don't give up"* (Galatians 6:7-9).

This gets back to a basic understanding about God. He loves people, yet He will not change the reality of His perfection. The laws of the universe reflect this fact. As followers, we cannot escape the truth that the Lord does not change the consequences for His children. He loves us too much to sit back and allow us to destroy ourselves without plenty of opportunity to change.

Daily obedience is far more important to God than any heroic feat or major accomplishment.

The prophet Samuel tried to teach this to King Saul when he said, *"Obedience is better than sacrifice..."* (1 Samuel 15:22).

Most parents agree they would rather have children who joyfully obey all year long instead of trying to make-up every Mother's or Father's Day.

To define greatness in the Kingdom is to understand that obedience to Christ is central to a dynamic relationship with God. Dressing up for Easter services, asking for forgiveness and placing an offering in the plate as it goes by, is sometimes a slap in the face of the Almighty. It looks more like religion than relationship!

Obeying Christ daily is not about developing some kind of spiritual "to-do" list or completing a few "Jesus chores." It is more concerned with cultivating a thriving alliance with the Lord through His Spirit and His Word so we can navigate through daily life following the directions of Christ in every situation. When this is the case, the Spirit guides you through the day prompting you in your relationships, ethics, troubles and opportunities.

Obedience is the ultimate expression of love for Christ.

How can a person know if they love God more than the enticements offered by the world? We are able to measure our heart for the Lord by the way we obey Him, love His ways, and our desire to play a part in His plan to redeem mankind. John said, *"Loving God means keeping his commandments, and his commandments are not burdensome. For every child of God defeats this evil world, and we achieve this victory through our faith. And who can win this battle against the world? Only those who believe that Jesus is the Son of God"* (1 John 5:3-5).

Imagine a planet free from violence—where kids can go out and play without fear of harm. Visualize a place where there is plenty of enriching, healthy activity without the threat of greed and tension between people. Think of an environment void of illness and disease. This is the new heaven and the new earth that will one day represent Christ's redeeming work. How hard is this to love?

Obedience is simply agreeing that God's path and His plans for the future are the only way to live. It is a lifestyle and commitment to remain in His love and to be considered His friend. The apostle John understood what Jesus began 2,000 years ago when he recorded Jesus' words: *"When you obey my commandments, you remain in my love, just as I obey my Father's commandments and remain in his love...You are my friends if you do what I command"* (John 15:10,14).

PUTTING IT INTO PRACTICE

Identify which of the following two statements is most true for you, then discuss it with those who are willing to engage in the topic.

1. I try to be a good Christian by learning and doing what's right to the best of my ability.
2. I try to integrate my relationship with Christ with every activity, person, place or situation.

Memorize John 15:14 and repeat it to yourself often during this week's schedule of activities.

POINTS TO PONDER

- Name several factors which you consider to be weak foundations for a strong spiritual life.
- According to God's Word, what are the consequences for disobedience?
- In your personal experience, how have you demonstrated trust and obedience to the Lord?

96

~ 19 ~
UNDERSTAND FAILURE

*Dear brothers and sisters, not many of
you should become teachers in the church, for
we who teach will be judged more strictly. Indeed,
we all make many mistakes. For if we could control
our tongues, we would be perfect and could
also control ourselves in every other way.*

– JAMES 3:1-2

Like many, I strive to make Christ central in my life. One of the areas the Lord has been moving me toward is the improvement of my physical and emotional well-being. I consider myself a former athlete—let me emphasize the word "former."

I have learned that without competitive sports I don't know how to challenge my body. I have also discovered that my physical conditioning has much to do with my emotional health. As a result, I have come to realize that I need to relearn what it means to be physically and emotionally healthy. This is humbling for me to admit, yet nonetheless true.

Recently, I was reading a book on health and strength training given to me by one of the emerging leaders in our church and decided to "brush up" on the subject of weightlifting. One re-occurring phrase in this section jumped off the pages: "Repeat this 8 to 12 times or failure." The author was referring to exercise repetitions, but the word "failure" caught my attention. After I gathered myself from an immediate and private protest against this word it began to make more sense to me within the context it was used.

The next day I was practicing one of the exercises prescribed in the book and was getting close to losing strength when those words "8 to 12 times or failure" popped into my head again. Now they made more sense than ever. I don't think he meant to say "8 to 12 times or 50 if you can." I believe he was suggesting, "Do at least 8, or perhaps think about lowering the amount of weight. See if you can do 12 or more, but if you can do 50, try heavier weights." As I finished my exercise—"failing" to accomplish my goals for the morning—I realized once again that failure is in the path of success.

As a Follower of Christ, What Does it Mean to Fail?

From a Christian perspective, failure is falling short in the attempt to do good.

To actively seek to do that which is evil does not constitute failure—it is perverted ambition. The Christian perspective of failure assumes that one is walking in the right direction, but has stumbled or fallen.

This is important to understand. If you stumble you are not out of the race. If you fall you are not dead and without God's restoring hand. Yes, there are consequences, but most of them come from the human realm, not from heaven. This means God understands that people have high expectations and little redeeming values to nourish those demands. The Lord's expectations are higher than ours, but Jesus' ministry is the redeeming activity which gives "failures" forgiveness and hope.

If you are a leader in the church, please recognize the difference between stumbling in your duties and faltering in the elementary virtues and values of Christ.

Leaders make mistakes in decision-making, strategies and the handling of difficult people. From these errors they become more humble, wiser and better leaders. But to waver in the virtues and disciplines of Christ bring the consequences of demotion and loss of respect. It is why James explains: *"Dear brothers and sisters, not many of you should become teachers in the church, for we who teach will be judged more strictly"* (James 3:1).

If you are going to preach something, you'd better practice it:

- If you preach tithing, you'd better be a tither.
- If you preach sharing your faith, you'd better be sharing your faith.
- If your preach forgiveness, you'd better forgive.

These are elementary to faith.

From a Christian perspective, failure is the result of running out of strength.

As followers of Christ, we take our *lives* seriously without taking *ourselves* too seriously. We know we exist for God's purposes and He wants us actively engaged with those objectives, but we are only human and need to rely upon Him more than we depend upon ourselves.

Failure, then, should be defined as a mistake. It is a learning opportunity not a condemned ending. As in physical strength building, what we fail at today we will succeed in tomorrow if we continue to show up and work out.

We run out of energy for many reasons—which should be understood as they are occurring. We need not be people of gloom and doom, but men and women who can recognize how our humanity was created to participate with the divine nature. Peter's insightful words shed light on this subject: *"By his divine power, God has given us everything we need for living a godly life. We have received all of this by coming to know him, the one who called us to himself by means of his marvelous glory and excellence. And because of his glory and excellence, he has given us great and precious promises. These are the promises that enable you to share his divine nature and escape the world's corruption caused by human desires"* (2 Peter 1:3-4).

There are normal, human reasons we run out of strength—not always as a result of sin. We need to remember that Jesus, who was without sin, still became hungry, thirsty and tired. So we can see how sharing in the divine nature does not override the normal aspects of human need.

We become weary when we fail to take care of ourselves. At times we make mistakes because we have allowed our emotions to get out of whack—which usually impacts the way we speak. Our words almost always uncover our inner condition.

How do our emotions get messed up? Typically, by neglecting the day-to-day needs of our body and mind. Are we resting, eating properly, laughing enough, learning, etc.? Are we in fellowship with people who build us up? Sometimes we can find the answer to mistakes by examining our daily lives.

We can also grow weary when we are going through difficult times. It may involve our loved ones, or can be a result of challenges in the workplace: mergers, down-sizing, etc. Perhaps we have been disappointed by those we counted on. Health problems can create havoc, not just in the body but also in our spirit and outlook on life. What about divorce or a death in the family? Can it get any worse? These possibilities bring us to our next reason for failure or loss of strength.

From a Christian perspective, failure is realized when we do not rely on the strength provided by Christ.

There is a point when consistent failure demonstrates one of two things: (1) we are attempting to take action without God or (2) the Lord is trying to get our attention. Usually both are true at the same time. Repeated failure indicates a life walking away from God's purposes.

The inability to trust the Father during extreme difficulty reveals that our inner investments into this world are greater than what we invest in a relationship with Christ. Paul reminds us from his own experience about the strength available to us in Christ when he said, *"For I can do everything through Christ, who gives me strength. Even so, you have done well to share with me in my present difficulty"* (Philippians 4:13-14).

This is the participation with the divine nature to which Peter was referring. There will be days we go far beyond simply being tired and in need of refreshing—and may experience valleys with shadows and images of doom. But be encouraged that through a genuine fellowship with Christ you will feel His nearness and strength to finish the race. You may stumble, fall and make mistakes, yet the nourishment of Christ will pick you up and help you continue until your days on earth are finally completed.

PUTTING IT INTO PRACTICE

At what have you failed and become too discouraged to get up and try again? What is in your past or your present you are too ashamed to share? Where do you need help?

Ask your Heavenly Father to guide you in the truthful answers to these questions. As He reveals these truths, share them with those you believe should hear your story, so they can encourage and release you from the dark closet of secrets. If you need guidance, ask for help—and keep asking until you find a place or person who can pick you up and dust you off. Start again and remember as a follower you can stumble and you can fall, but from God's perspective, failure is impossible.

POINTS TO PONDER

- Recall what seemed like a major setback at the time—but proved to be God moving you forward.
- According to Scripture, how does God see our mistakes and human errors?
- In what ways have you felt the Father's hand of strength and guidance during your times of trials?

~20~
SERVE

I remind you to fan into flames the spiritual gift
God gave you when I laid my hands on you. For God
has not given us a spirit of fear and timidity, but
of power, love, and self-discipline.
— 2 TIMOTHY 1:6-7

One of the funniest scenes I have witnessed was played out on the big screen. In this particular romantic comedy, the main character is portrayed as a type of Murphy's Law expert. No matter what he tries to do something always goes wrong. One series of events found him standing face-to-face with a female boarding agent who was taking passenger tickets at the gate.

I am laughing again as I type these words. Let me describe the setting first. There is not one soul in the boarding area other than our main character and this great actress playing the part of Sheriff of Boarding Pass Regulations and Orderly Would-Be Passenger Conduct. Our main character approaches the woman with a pleasant greeting and attempts to hand her his boarding pass. She takes a look at the ticket and tells the passenger they are not yet boarding his row (remember, no one else is in sight). After a short appeal process by our star, she denies his request and asks him to step back and wait for her to call his row.

Confused and feeling persecuted, he steps back and waits in a line of one. About five seconds later, she calls his row for boarding. Still looking around in confusion, he approaches with caution to the pleasant greeting of the same woman, whose attitude has drastically changed. She accepts his boarding pass and welcomes him aboard. I am still chuckling at the memory of this short but insightful clip that pokes fun at a type of customer service which often just doesn't make sense.

Followers of Jesus can laugh at this scenario as long as it doesn't represent our attitude when we serve one another and those God places around us.

WHAT DOES CHRISTIAN SERVICE LOOK LIKE?

Serve others as you would serve Jesus.

I hear it everywhere I go. Frankly, I am guilty of saying it myself. We are often dissatisfied and complain over the quality of service we receive whether from a merchant, restaurant, school, government, or the local church. I guess we should not be complainers, but there can be some truth to our griping. It seems it is difficult to find good service these days!

With all the great business books on the market, I still think there is room for one more. The name of the book and the writing on the first and only page would read: "Serve Your Customers as You Enjoy Being Served," and I believe if the reader practiced this advice, 80% of their success would be guaranteed. While some people really just don't care, most of us do.

If you are going to follow Jesus you will find yourself serving others just as He did. When God's Son encountered human need, He wanted people to experience the true nature of the Father. He desired to demonstrate what heaven on earth might look like—and for us to understand that one of our purposes is to bring heaven to earth in the form of service to our fellow man. Jesus explained: *"...the King will say to those on his right, 'Come, you who are blessed by my Father, inherit the Kingdom prepared for you from the creation of the world. For I was hungry, and you fed me. I was thirsty, and you gave me a drink. I was a stranger, and you invited me into your home. I was naked, and you gave me clothing. I was sick, and you cared for me. I was in prison, and you visited me.' Then these righteous ones will reply, 'Lord, when did we ever see you hungry and feed you? Or thirsty and give you something to drink? Or a stranger and show you hospitality? Or naked and give you clothing? When did we ever see you sick or in prison and visit you?' And the King will say, 'I tell you the truth, when you did it to one of the least of these my brothers and sisters, you were doing it to me!"* (Matthew 25:34-40).

Notice how many of Jesus' examples are as easy as basic human kindness to those who are thirsty or need temporary shelter. Then we see some who challenge our servant's heart at a deeper level. He speaks of individuals who are homeless and without clothing, which will require larger sums of money and inconvenience. Then He mentions caring for the sick and even criminals.

Jesus is calling us to represent Him in *all* we do. We are to be His hands, His feet, His words and His actions. In order to serve others as we would serve Jesus we will have to exhibit a sense of compassion and excellence because we exemplify the very nature of heaven.

Serve others with the gifts God has given you.

The Bible has listed a variety of abilities we have come to know as spiritual gifts. Many of these are given to you at your physical birth, while others are bestowed at your spiritual birth. You may be given these at appointed times and places so you can serve in an unusual situation. Paul describes this mystery: *"There are different kinds of spiritual gifts, but the same Spirit is the source of them all. There are different kinds of service, but we serve the same Lord. God works in different ways, but it is the same God who does the work in all of us. A spiritual gift is given to each of us so we can help each other"* (1 Corinthians 12:4-7).

Instead of listing all the spiritual gifts we are able to pull out of the Scriptures, it is more important to understand the purpose and source of them.

Spiritual gifts are given to build up the Body of Christ. This is done both by adding to the Body and helping it grow stronger. Notice also from the verses above that the gifts come from God the Spirit. It is essential to recognize that God does different things through different people. We should not assume everyone is a gifted teacher or administrator. However, we should receive each other's gift as a ministry coming from the Holy Spirit. The point being, the church needs *all* the gifts, so we should appreciate each member's willingness to share what the Lord has presented.

Serve others with your total package.

You have received spiritual gifts, plus you either already have or will learn skills throughout your days. In addition, you encounter life-shaping experiences, some difficult, some pleasant, but both mold the architecture of your soul. Your personality plays a vital role, as do your dreams and passions—and you have many available resources.

All these combine to make you the unique person you are, and when packaged together, they will present a dynamic opportunity to serve Christ by serving others.

Perhaps one of the most life-changing experiences that can bring healing stems from our past hurts. Paul was aware of this fact: *"All praise to God, the Father of our Lord Jesus Christ. God is our merciful Father and the source of all comfort. He comforts us in all our troubles so that we can comfort others. When they are troubled, we will be able to give them the same comfort God has given us"* (2 Corinthians 1:3-4).

PUTTING IT INTO PRACTICE

We need to serve others, starting where there is an obvious need. The best way to learn what you are able to offer will come from learning while doing. Don't allow a lack of on-hand know-how to inhibit or stop you from taking the first step. Start somewhere and learn how God will enrich and grow you through serving.

POINTS TO PONDER

- Which spiritual gift do you already possess which needs fanning the flame?
- In what areas have you been called to serve?
- What needs do you see around you that are still unfilled? How could you help?

~ 21 ~
Surrender

And so, dear brothers and sisters, I plead with you to give your bodies to God because of all he has done for you. Let them be a living and holy sacrifice—the kind he will find acceptable. This is truly the way to worship him. Don't copy the behavior and customs of this world, but let God transform you into a new person by changing the way you think. Then you will learn to know God's will for you, which is good and pleasing and perfect.
— Romans 12:1-2

Even if you don't know the name Aron Ralston, you may recall hearing his story. He is the young climber who was trapped in Utah's Bluejohn Canyon when an 800-pound boulder suddenly shifted and crushed his right wrist and arm. He was trapped against the canyon wall.

For six days Aron struggled to free himself—all the while fighting off dehydration and hypothermia. Surprised to be alive this long, thoughts of suicide previously dismissed began to re-enter his mind.

In a fable-like manner, he discovered the hope of freedom with the thought of amputation. Small steps of experimentation followed. The procedure began even in the midst of delusions. If death was sure, he was going to meet it with action. It all began with the breaking of bones by twisting back and forth, poking and cutting, and observing. After forty minutes of this, he continued to learn more of the body's mysterious engineering. The smallest nerve endings sent shocks of pain up his shoulder. After a few minutes of recovery he continued.

The intense pain was overcome by hope and adrenaline. These are his exact words depicting, in my view, the power of surrender: "It is

11:32 A.M., Thursday, May 1, 2003. For the second time in my life, I am being born. This time I am being delivered from the canyon's pink womb, where I have been incubating. This time I am a grown adult, and I understand the significance and power of this birth as none of us can when it happens the first time."[1]

What Aron is describing is extremely spiritual. In order to experience life as God intends, one needs to be free. However, freedom is thwarted by the things we have not totally surrendered—what we are not willing to give up for fear they are better than what awaits us on the other side.

Finally, Aron breaks free. This is how he expresses his euphoria: "I AM FREE! This is the most intense feeling of my life."[2]

WHAT IS "SURRENDER" TO THE CHRISTIAN?

Surrender is to turn your entire life over to Christ.

We hold onto "things"—money, material possessions, relationships, rights, hurts, grudges and privileges—out of weakness, not strength. What a contrast when we turn our lives over to the Lord and allow Him to guide us in every way. He provides us with the ability to earn wages and directs the use of these funds. Suddenly, the possessions in our hands are for His purposes. Even how we interact with people is learned from Christ.

Financial problems, due to our lack of patience and greed, will fade as we learn that having Christ is all we need. The Lord promises to provide "all things" as we surrender to Him. Jesus says: *"So don't worry about these things, saying, 'What will we eat? What will we drink? What will we wear?' These things dominate the thoughts of unbelievers, but your heavenly Father already knows all your needs. Seek the Kingdom of God above all else, and live righteously, and he will give you everything you need. So don't worry about tomorrow, for tomorrow will bring its own worries. Today's trouble is enough for today"* (Matthew 6:31-34).

Relationships are always a challenge because there are at least two people involved. However, as we submit ourselves to the Lord, He helps us become wise in all of our relational endeavors. When we resist or fail to yield to God's Son, we choose to live in the weakness of our humanity, not in the strength of the resurrected Christ living within.

Surrender provides freedom from destructive living.

The ways of the world are first "numbing," then destructive. Humans without the presence of Christ are inwardly confused about why they exist and why life seems to have no clear purpose. The first phase of expressing such confusion is denial—which deadens feeling.

Some people numb their unhappy inner person with the pursuit of personal goals meant to satisfy and define. Others dull their senses with recreational overload, or they chase money and possessions. The old adage, "Sex, Drugs, and Rock and Roll" is alive and well although it takes many forms. In excess, alcohol, entertainment, and the social scene echo the loneliness of the soul. These are the "behaviors" and "customs" of the world to which Paul is speaking in Romans 12:2.

Thank the Lord, there is a better way. It is a life-long process of transformation which starts with the re-birthing of a soul by faith into God's family. The renovation continues as we live and learn to trust the way Christ leads.

Discarding the old rags of this world and replacing them with the new wardrobe from heaven is a delightful and rewarding process. You have clothed yourselves with a brand new nature that is continually being renewed as you learn more and more about Christ, who created this new nature within you (Colossians 3:10).

Surrendered men and women experience ongoing encouragement from the Lord, which builds up the believer and creates the strength to accept earthly realities while looking ahead to the promises of God. The need for numbing fades as our desire grows for more of Christ.

Surrender allows Christ to change your way of thinking.

Change does not happen without a new desire, which gives you a fresh perspective and creates energy where once there was none. It is described as *regeneration*—a word that paints a picture of God's process of change. When God regenerates a soul He plants new passions and perspectives which produce divine strength and power. Without God's new creation within there is no hope for change.

Transformation in behavior is linked to altered thinking. For example, armies retreat when they believe a battle cannot be won, but they pursue when confidence is high and the cause is worth the sacrifice of life. On the other hand, surrender occurs when there is nowhere to run and continuing the current behavior will bring only death.

Regeneration of the mind is in effect when a follower of Jesus Christ no longer views any human as a threat to their well-being and happiness. The mind has been invaded by Christ and optimism replaces pessimism. We can have a positive outlook because no matter what today's events seem to say, the final outcome will be for God's purposes.

There is no hopeless thinking in the mind of a growing follower of Christ—only *good* is possible and imminent. The apostle Peter reminds us of the new world God is creating: *"But we are looking forward to the new heavens and new earth he has promised, a world filled with God's righteousness"* (2 Peter 3:13).

This encourages the regenerated mind—which does not doubt, but eagerly awaits this new indwelling. It is in the *knowing* that one is enlightened and empowered. This is why the recreated believer gives all to Christ—understanding everything is about God.

PUTTING IT INTO PRACTICE

Every day, surrender your body and mind to the Lord. Give up your rights and yield complete control to Him. Perhaps you can identify an area of your life where this submission has not yet occurred. Ask the Lord to change you—and He will if you do your part. What is required?

Step one: Turn this area over to Him with a simple but sincere prayer. Step two: Seek out solid teaching to keep you from sliding back into self-destructive thinking and behavior patterns. Step three: Be ready and willing to help.

POINTS TO PONDER

- What have been the most difficult things to surrender to Christ?
- How has becoming a believer changed your thinking?
- Give an example of how a transformed mind affects behavior.

[1] Ralston, Aron, *Between A Rock and A Hard Place*, New York: Atria Books, pp. 284-5.
[2] ibid, p.285

~ 22 ~
STRIVE FOR SIMPLICITY

...true godliness with contentment is itself
great wealth. After all, we brought nothing with
us when we came into the world, and we can't take anything
with us when we leave it. So if we have enough food and
clothing, let us be content. But people who long to be rich fall
into temptation and are trapped by many foolish and harmful
desires that plunge them into ruin and destruction. For the love
of money is the root of all kinds of evil. And some people,
craving money, have wandered from the true faith and
pierced themselves with many sorrows.
– 1 TIMOTHY 6:6-10

Like most young couples, Rhonda and I started our marriage with very few earthly possessions. We had plenty of energy, a good amount of faith in God, and lots of young love to give to each other. Our one-bedroom apartment in California was clean and neat—with an ice chest in the spot where we would someday place a refrigerator. We had a bench press without the weights that served as a television stand for our 13" color screen. My parents gave us a bed and we owned an old moped and a green Buick. We both worked at least one job and were still in college.

For entertainment we simply spent time together, or with our friends at church and in the apartment complex where we lived. We also would hang out at the mall, buy an ice cream cone, people-watch, and had no problem finding things to do. If we could afford it, we would drive to the beach and enjoy the sand, sun and water. I also spent a lot of time playing on various sports teams for fun. This was one of the areas in my life I was unwilling to give up, despite my love for Rhonda. In time, however, I learned it was one of my earthly gods that needed to be destroyed.

We regularly attended church services and occasionally participated in the young married couples' Bible study group. People were kind to us. These were simple, good days, but like the echo of my dad's words, "Where did all the time go?"

WHY SIMPLICITY IS IMPORTANT

Simplicity removes unnecessary stress.

Think of what God has already generously provided: sunsets, sunrises, oceans, streams, lakes and mountains—plus friends, stories and imagination. These are the simple things of life created for our enjoyment..

Simplicity is an attitude. The Lord encourages us to dream and to work, but living one day at a time makes the process memorable and significant. It is much like the difference between driving on a busy highway or meandering down a scenic country road; they are two completely different journeys.

Every person can practice the discipline of simplicity. It is not some naive longing for simpler days. As we will see, it is the way of Christ. In the process, affluent people and pressured executives will discover that most unhealthy stress is self-inflicted. The poor and middle class will eventually realize the uselessness of constantly striving to get ahead while missing out on all God's simple pleasures along the way.

King Solomon was the richest man of his day and at least one of the wealthiest in all of history, yet he grew to appreciate a life of simplicity: *"Some people work wisely with knowledge and skill, then must leave the fruit of their efforts to someone who hasn't worked for it. This, too, is meaningless, a great tragedy. So what do people get in this life for all their hard work and anxiety? Their days of labor are filled with pain and grief; even at night their minds cannot rest. It is all meaningless"* (Ecclesiastes 2:21-23).

Solomon's words should make us think and question. How much

money and "stuff" does one person or family really need? At what point does an individual's schedule, inventory of possessions and income actually create stress instead of relieve it?

I am not a wealthy man by the standards in North America, nor was I born into abundance. However, I have many friends who are rich and I've noticed that most of them struggle with the same issues everyone else experiences, plus one more. It seems nearly everyone they know has their hands out!

Also, while many are trying to obtain more riches, the wealthy are attempting just as hard not to lose theirs. This vicious cycle can only be stopped by the discipline of simplicity.

Simplicity makes life more enjoyable.

Millions are tempted by the media to buy the newest and latest—even though the older model still works just fine. The discipline of simplicity responds with a series of rational questions. First, "Why spend money on this when what I have operates perfectly. Second, "If this new version was not available, would I know the difference?" Third, "Do I even need the old model? What would my life be like if I got rid of this thing all together?"

The other day I watched a normally calm young person become very agitated and angry with his laptop computer because it wasn't responding in the split-second manner to which he was accustomed. On a recent news broadcast, I learned that a university study has revealed a growing lack of patience among most people. The study's hypothesis suggests that while the world moves faster through great strides in technology, the human is slowly losing touch with the reality of time and has grown dependent upon the power and speed of the microchip.

Most seminaries now have courses which examine the ethics of technology within the realm of Christian living and ministry. This is a legitimate concern in light of its impact upon relationships, privacy and access to all kinds of destructive behaviors. Artificial intelligence has the potential to delay or destroy the ability of young people to live an enjoyable life full of relationships and problem-solving skills.

Dallas Willard, in his book, *The Spirit of the Disciplines,* says, [People who have entered into simplicity] "...easily put all demands that come to them in 'their place' and deal harmoniously, peacefully, and confidently with complexities of life that seem incomprehensible to others, for they know what they are doing."

The positive potential of technology is undeniable, but it can never replace the powerful outcome of an attitude of simple living.

Simplicity is the way of Christ.

It is interesting to consider God's chosen path for Jesus to walk. He could have come at a time in history that was most convenient and pampering to the human body. He could have been born into great wealth and influence. However, God chose the opposite. Christ came through a young, simple, and godly woman. He was born in humble circumstances in a town not greatly known.

If the life of Christ were made into a movie reflecting the American dream, it would be a great beginning. The screen writers would then demonstrate resolve and persistence as Jesus would climb the ladder of success. He would become famous and accumulate great wealth and power. As you know, this was not the way of Christ. Instead Jesus had simplicity of purpose and lifestyle. As He said: *"For even the Son of Man came not to be served but to serve others and to give his life as a ransom for many"* (Matthew 20:28).

The Lord never taught that money, commerce or to be born into wealth was evil. Rather, these can be used by God for His purpose—to redeem the world through His Son, Jesus Christ.

PUTTING IT INTO PRACTICE

Identify at least one area of your life (a luxury, an activity, an ambition, etc.) that is creating more stress than enjoyment. What are you going to do about this?

Name one gift provided by God (friends, sunsets, leisurely walks, etc.) which you need to start enjoying again.

List ways in which Christ lived a simple life. To follow His example, which of these will you begin to practice this week?

POINTS TO PONDER

- Contrast the lifestyle of your parents and yourself. What simple pleasures were important to them?
- If you were asked to eliminate one modern-day invention, what would it be? Why?
- What steps will you take to carve out a "quiet time" to spend with the Lord?

~ 23 ~
PRAY

Don't worry about anything; instead,
pray about everything. Tell God what you
need, and thank him for all he has done.
– PHILIPPIANS 4:6

I set myself up! In an attempt to be a good friend, mentor and pastor, I took a small group of young men on an outdoor adventure. My purpose: to build deeper relationships and learn more about the Christian journey through the beauty and challenges of a wilderness quest involving camping, rock climbing, and white water rafting.

We took a professional along to be our guide and instructor. His job was to teach us how to accomplish these adventures in an educated and skilled manner, and he caught our attention by the way he conducted himself with expertise and honor. However, we did not realize that he was part wild-man!

While rafting, he asked if we wanted to do something crazy. How are "macho men" supposed to answer such a question? We responded with words absent of fear or concern. This was my first mistake. You may be wondering why I didn't say "This was OUR first mistake." You'll see.

We put our raft on the shore as the guide directed, then he asked us to follow him out into the raging river. At this particular point there was a series of large boulders protruding from the very active current—with no dry spots on the surfaces.

Gingerly, we hopped, walked, jumped and crawled out to the location where our guide was standing. He stood on the last boulder, and turned toward us and began to explain this crazy stunt. As I recall, he was shouting due to the noise of the current crashing against the rocks.

This is what I remember him saying, "We are going to jump into the rapids one at a time, and when it is your turn remember these things: Hold your breath because you are going to travel about 100 yards before you can breathe again. Do not struggle unless you want to drown. Don't try to float to the surface because the current will not allow it. Keep your legs up so they won't strike a rock. When you come up at that bend down there, swim like mad toward shore because you don't want to travel any further down without a boat—believe me!"

Just as I thought this was all a joke to scare us—he turned and jumped into the river.

There was a collective gasp; we could not believe our eyes. We focused on the proposed direction of his destination for what seemed like forever. Then finally, we saw a body pop up, flailing his arms until he reached the shore. I looked back toward the guys to find every eye focused on me as if they were saying, "It's your turn, Mr. Leader."

HOW IS PRAYER LIKE JUMPING INTO A DANGEROUS RIVER?

Prayer removes worry.

From personal experience and from listening to others for years, prayer does not come naturally to most of us unless we are in a life or death situation. Some are spiritually gifted in this area, but most are not. However, the longer we follow Jesus, the more we pray and the less we worry.

Now it was my turn, and I jumped into the river! The water was cold, turbulent and shocking. My first impulse was to react, and my survival instincts screamed, "Get to the surface!" But then I remembered his words, "Do not struggle, keep your legs up and hold your breath."

The first few seconds were difficult, but as the second hand continued to tick in my head, I began to relax and wonder how long I would have to hold my breath. I realized how powerful his words were to me at that specific moment and place. It reminds me of a proverb which speaks of the importance of truthful and encouraging words,

"Worry weighs a person down; an encouraging word cheers a person up" (Proverbs 12:25).

I concentrated on not struggling, keeping my legs up and holding my breath. Without realizing, I was communicating in my mind to our wilderness guide. I was speaking back to him what he spoke to me earlier, and the more I did this the less anxious I became. I trusted him; I had no other rational choice. Here's the point, his words of truth kept me from doing something stupid, which usually starts with worry.

Prayer aligns you with God's Spirit.

Christ promises peace in exchange for anxiousness. Remember, God is *always* at rest, so when we experience His peace it doesn't automatically make human sense. As Paul writes: *"Don't worry about anything; instead, pray about everything. Tell God what you need, and thank him for all he has done. Then you will experience God's peace, which exceeds anything we can understand. His peace will guard your hearts and minds as you live in Christ Jesus"* (Philippians 4:6-7).

To know God's rest is not some kind of divine spell or mental trance; it is a sense of calm which accompanies the knowledge God is in control. He is not caught off guard by the circumstances and needs brought to Him in prayer. He already knew, but He gives you His peace when you tell Him about your troubles.

Have you ever known a person who had a calming affect on a situation which seemed chaotic? What and how did this individual communicate? Usually it was in a calm, reassuring voice with a fully engaged demeanor that reflects a good balance of confidence and compassion. Their comments may sound like this: "I understand your concern and can see why you are upset. Let's think about this together and I am sure there will be a positive outcome."

A good leader is sincere with his words, just the way Christ is when we talk to Him. He aligns us with His Spirit, causing us to think clearly and confidently.

Prayer makes you laugh again.

Back on our adventure, just about the time I started worrying again, the river spewed me above the surface of the water. Immediately, I remembered my own version of the guide's instruction "SWIM LIKE HECK!"

There are times in prayer when God not only provides peace, but also instruction. And when you receive His direction, there is no doubt or second guessing, because it came from Him.

When I reached the shore, I started laughing uncontrollably. I exclaimed, "That was amazing! What was I thinking? That was scary! That was crazy!"

Looking back at my life and the various battles within, I can smile and see how God had His hand on my every move, even when I demonstrated little faith. I appreciate the following verse of Scripture because it gives me the permission to tell God that even though I know I should not be apprehensive, I am. *"Search me, O God, and know my heart; test me and know my anxious thoughts"* (Psalm 139:23 NIV).

It's like saying, "Lord, I know better, and I come to You now because I need to be reminded of Your faithfulness so I can rejoice and laugh again!"

PUTTING IT INTO PRACTICE

If you have the gift of intercession, this lesson was simply a confirmation of your experience as a follower of Jesus. But if you are more like me, you need some tips.

First, in order to become a person of prayer you must be well-acquainted with Scripture. Those who pray often usually know the Bible. This is true because much of prayer is saying back to God what He has already spoken to us in His Word.

Second, praying isn't an activity I schedule on my calendar— it has to become my lifestyle. In order to do this I have come to realize Christ is with me *always,* because He is omnipresent and dwells within me. Therefore, I speak to Him all day long about everything. I converse with Him like I speak to my friends, whether it is in my mind or aloud.

Third, several times a week, as I am reading my Bible, I write out a prayer in my reading/prayer journal. This usually relates to what I have read that day.

Fourth, for some people it is more encouraging to pray in a small group of trusted friends.

Fifth, some find it very helpful to make a list of prayer requests others have shared and commit to pray for these concerns for as long as it takes. There are many excellent books on the topic, but I find practice is more profitable than research in this matter. Pick out one or more of the ideas we have mentioned and put them into practice. Share what you are doing with someone who cares.

POINTS TO PONDER

- Recall a time when pray relieved your anxiety, worry or fear.
- In your communion and fellowship with the Lord, describe how God speaks to you.
- What do you believe is the proper balance between presenting your requests to the Lord, and spending time worshiping and praising Him?

~ 24 ~
WITNESS

But you will receive power when the Holy
Spirit comes upon you. And you will be my witnesses,
telling people about me everywhere...
– ACTS 1:8

It happened over one of those three-day weekends. We were driving over to a friend's house for some fun and fellowship when my wife Rhonda warned me with a loud and effective "Jim, watch out!"

Crossing over the middle dividing line of a two way street and heading right toward us was a small compact car. As I swerved out of the way, I caught a glimpse of the driver, who looked like he was asleep. Unfortunately, my position on the road completely eclipsed the oncoming car from the sight of the driver behind me and in the next lane over.

The facts get a little blurry from here. It seemed like I looked in my rearview mirror, then through my driver's side window as I swerved, and heard the head-on crash of these two vehicles at the same time. In a flash, I turned my swerve into a U-turn and started back toward the accident. Rhonda told the kids to stay in the vehicle and we both got out of our family van as fast as we could.

Without a thought, I went straight to the car that was traveling just behind us. Thinking back on it, I suppose I had already decided who was innocent and who was guilty. My mercy spilled out on the "innocent" first. I saw a little girl in the back seat as I opened her door. I will never forget her name and what I saw as Mary looked to me for comfort.

This little girl, maybe eight years old, looked me straight in the eyes and asked, "Am I going to die?" She had no visual trace of injury until her mouth spoke those words. Her face was split right down the middle from her nose up to the top of her forehead. I'm sorry for the graphic details, but this is what took place.

Rhonda and I were there for some time trying to offer whatever comfort we could. Mary's mother and father, who were in the front seat, were both hurt and floating in and out of consciousness. The driver responsible crawled out of his car bloodied and dragging a broken leg. We found out later that he was under the influence of a variety of illegal drugs.

WHAT ARE THE RESPONSIBILITIES OF A WITNESS?

A witness simply tells what he or she knows to be true.
"Did you see what happened?"—this is the basic question asked of a witness.

Sadly, some will avoid answering by fleeing the scene or denying any first-hand knowledge of the event. Common reasons given for not getting involved are to avoid the hassle of lost time and fear of personal liability. However, most would view these as cowardly excuses. Some might suggest that such a person is a disgrace to society. All we require from witnesses is to tell what they saw or experienced. Most of us are not only willing, we are eager because we know the information is important.

The first disciples of Jesus were to be a witness to the resurrection of Christ from the dead. In doing so, the Lord promised that as they became witnesses, power from heaven would fill their being and validate their story so that many would be encouraged to trust in Christ as Savior of the world. The church and the Good News were birthed by God through Jesus, the Holy Spirit, and His witnesses. His church continues this work today based on the simple but profound event of the resurrection of Christ. Jesus prayed that we would be united with Him and those early witnesses as we continued spreading the message.

In the words of our Savior, *"Just as you sent me into the world, I am sending them into the world. And I give myself as a holy sacrifice for them so they can be made holy by your truth. I am praying not only for these disciples but also for all who will ever believe in me through their message. I pray that they will all be one, just as you and I are one—as you are in me, Father, and I am in you. And may they be in us so that the world will believe you sent me"* (John 17:18-21).

Unity is created when we listen to one voice—the unmistakable voice of Jesus. And power is provided through obedience to what the Lord requires—to be witnesses.

At the accident scene, we did not wait for the police to ask us what we had seen. We went to them, as most people would. An injustice had occurred and three people minding their own business were seriously injured by a man high on drugs behind the wheel of a car. If the timing of the events were just a couple of seconds different, they would be helping us instead of the reverse.

A witness helps reconcile the truth.

If the story isn't properly told, certain pieces of truth remain missing and lives may hang in the balance. Sometimes a witness is discredited because the account doesn't reconcile with other evidence. This is why it is imperative for a witness to stick to the facts. If an observer tries to become more dramatic or visualize something which wasn't seen or experienced firsthand, it often creates more harm than good—not to mention the damage wrong assumptions can cause.

The story of a man born blind and healed by Jesus is one of the most remarkable examples of what a good witness does. The religious leaders are confused by Jesus' power and at odds with His methods, so they call the healed man into their presence to question him. You can read the rest: *"'I don't know whether he is a sinner,' the man replied. 'But I know this: I was blind, and now I can see!' 'But what did he do?' they asked. 'How did he heal you?' 'Look!' the man exclaimed. 'I told you once. Didn't you listen? Why do you want to hear it again? Do you want to become his disciples, too?' Then they cursed him and said, 'You are his disciple, but we are disciples of Moses! We know God spoke to Moses, but we don't even know where this man comes from.' 'Why, that's very strange!' the man replied. 'He healed my eyes, and yet you don't know where he comes from? We know that God doesn't listen to sinners, but he is ready to hear those who worship him and do his will. Ever since the world began, no one has been able to open the eyes of someone born blind. If this man were not from God, he couldn't have done it'"* (John 9:25-33).

With simple facts and logic, the man healed of blindness shares his story. This is exactly what God wants us to do.

Thankfully, after the accident, we learned that Mary and her parents fully recovered. I haven't seen or spoken to them since, but I can still testify to their story. The incident is forever part of my life and cannot be erased. So it is with the hope I have found in Jesus.

A witness carries great responsibility.

To keep silent and never share the Good News is not an option. The follower of Jesus carries within the body, spirit, and soul the most valuable information in all of creation. It is not ours to hoard, hide, or to give only to those we choose. Its origin is not bound in time for it was all part of God's plan. We hold within our being a sacred trust.

Scripture records, *"When they saw him, they worshiped him—but some of them doubted! Jesus came and told his disciples, 'I have been given all authority in heaven and on earth. Therefore, go and make disciples of all the nations, baptizing them in the name of the Father and the Son and the Holy Spirit. Teach these new disciples to obey all the commands I have given you. And be sure of this: I am with you always, even to the end of the age'"* (Matthew 28:17-20).

A follower of Christ is an active witness—and this behavior is normal. Fear is conquered by love for God and for His people. Power multiplies in the process.

PUTTING IT INTO PRACTICE

Write a one page description of how you came to believe in Jesus as the Savior of the world. Include the changes which have occurred since you placed your trust in Christ. Don't embellish and try to make it something it is not; just tell the truth. The transformation God has made in your life over the weeks, months or years may or may not seem significant to you. This is because you still long to experience more of Christ. However, other people can see the changes. Simply trust the Lord within you and tell what He has done.

Now think of individuals whom God has placed in your life who need to hear your story? Make a list of at least five people you will intentionally work with to develop a relationship, serve, and bring to the Father in prayer. Be aware of God's direction, and when He leads, be willing to follow. Do not be surprised if the Lord uses you differently in the life of each person.

Memorize Matthew 28:19-20. Cling to its truth. These verses are known as the Great Commission. Let the words flow through your being.

POINTS TO PONDER

- Describe a spiritual transformation you have personally witnessed in the life of a friend or someone you love.
- What details stand out in your mind?
- In your own words, explain what it means to you to be a witness for the Lord Jesus Christ?

BECOMING LIKE CHRIST

We often define good character as a person who is honest, diligent, forgiving, persevering, reliable, helpful and kind. Most of us strive to be this type of individual—not just on the outside but also inwardly.

Our desire is to be the "real deal"—a person of impeccable reputation and integrity. If we were to combine all these values together, we would have the description of the ideal human. He or she would be an authentic person, in line with God's original intent. This individual would be like a flawless diamond, and we would be able to enjoy the sparkle as well as the transparency.

Jesus is such a person. He was the perfect human being; God in the flesh. Yet, what draws us to Christ is His humility. Though He is God the Son, He lived among us and demonstrated what true godly character looks like on a daily basis.

The Almighty could have stopped at the Ten Commandments and simply said, "Consider yourself warned." But I am so glad that's not what He did. He became a Man, like us, so He could model what godliness looks like, then give us the ability to do the same through our rebirth and relationship with Him.

In the next 12 lessons we will consider how Christlike qualities can be applied in our daily lives. We should be able to walk away after completing this study with a better understanding of how Jesus Christ's character can reign within, radiate through and beyond us.

~ 25 ~
THE REAL YOU

*Now may the God of peace make you holy
in every way, and may your whole spirit and soul
and body be kept blameless until that day when
our Lord Jesus Christ comes again.*
– 1 THESSALONIANS 5:23

We were slowly making our way down the Andes of Bolivia. I was riding in the backseat of a 4-wheel drive vehicle, altered to better manage the rough terrain. Resting in my arms was a very ill little girl from one of the mountain villages. Her mother placed the child in the care of one of my colleagues, knowing that she would probably never see her daughter again. Without money, medical facilities or transportation, this mother saw no other option. So we took her sick child down the mountain to the city of Sucre, with the hopes of admitting her into a hospital.

We had been away from home for only a week, but it seemed like a season. I was tired, emotional, irritable, confused, frustrated, and depressed. I had not enjoyed a good meal, a decent night's rest or a shower. Instead, I was exposed to a primitive culture that communicated in several languages, none of which was English. These mountain villages lacked sanitary conditions, electricity, indoor plumbing, or any conveniences outside of surviving. I simply felt useless and lost.

My purpose for going was to observe the activity of a missionary, pitch in from time-to-time with my pastoral training and to help meet any other practical need. So we loaded equipment, handed out medicine, preached with the help of interpreters, conducted a wedding, mended wounds—and took turns caressing a dying baby girl as we made our way back home.

Many thoughts were racing through my mind as we continued to drive down the mountain, absorbing the bumps, the dust, and the consistent cries for help from the ailing child. I thought to myself, "Where is Jesus right now? I know we are His hands and His feet, but what good are they, if they cannot heal like Jesus can?"

I also entertained uneasy feelings about never getting back home to my family and church in Colorado. I thought about the overwhelming needs of people all around the world, while industrialized nations like the United States enjoy great comfort and wealth. I wondered why I was so blessed to be born in America.

As a "fixer," I also felt hopeless and powerless to help these people. When you harbor such feelings your mind begins to wander. I started thinking of my own family and their needs, contemplating what their future might be in the event of my death. These unsettling thoughts captured my imagination for hours, days, and even a few weeks. The "real me" was in conflict—and this is not always bad. During such soul-searching times, you often uncover new things about yourself and experience deep change.

Christ Alive in You

Paul prayed that the God of peace make us holy in every way, and *"...may your whole spirit and soul and body be kept blameless..."* (1 Thessalonians 5:23).

It's not by accident that he pens three words describing the human makeup: spirit, soul, and body. Perhaps this is why human beings are so complex! In order to begin operating like Jesus, it is helpful to understand how God designed us. Paul is not suggesting we are made of three separate entities, but he is describing an inner person comprised of spirit and soul, and an outer person, which is our body.

Your spirit is what makes you aware of God; it allows you to communicate with Him.

You do not have these abilities, however, until God's Spirit brings you to life. Paul explains this further: *"You were dead because of your sins and because your sinful nature was not yet cut away. Then God made you alive with Christ, for he forgave all our sins"* (Colossians 2:13).

We cannot respond to God unless He brings life to us—and until He gives us His Spirit we are dead. So when we respond to God's offer of forgiveness, we do so only by His grace. Therefore, life really does not begin until our spirit is united with the Spirit of God.

Once this happens, we have become new creations. Our renewed self desires to listen and obey the Spirit of God. This is what is meant by the phrase "the Christian walk." *"Since we are living by the Spirit, let us follow the Spirit's leading in every part of our lives"* (Galatians 5:25).

But there's a rub: This new way of living wars against what your body, mind, and emotions have believed and practiced in the past.

The opposite extreme of your reborn inner person is the cravings of your old nature—otherwise known as "the flesh."

We learned in school that our flesh receives information through five senses: hearing, sight, smell, taste, and touch. In other words, it interacts with our surroundings, the environment in which we live.

The apostle John describes accurately the war waging between the new nature and our old carnality: *"Do not love this world nor the things it offers you, for when you love the world, you do not have the love of the Father in you. For the world offers only a craving for physical pleasure, a craving for everything we see, and pride in our achievements and possessions. These are not from the Father, but are from this world. And this world is fading away, along with everything that people crave..."* (1 John 2:15-17).

The old appetites can be compelling memories, even though they are truly dead to the new inner person. The Bible teaches us two things about our decaying flesh. First, it has no power over us when we obey the Spirit of God. Second, it will always be with us while we are housed in our earthly bodies. This is why we call it a "war."

Though the evils of this world are ultimately dead and now colliding under the relentless weight of God's perfection and absolute will, our old sinful nature continues the struggle against our new Spirit-filled nature. The apostle Paul describes our conflict with these words: *"So I say, let the Holy Spirit guide your lives. Then you won't be doing what your sinful nature craves. The sinful nature wants to do evil, which is just the opposite of what the Spirit wants. And the Spirit gives us desires that are the opposite of what the sinful nature desires. These two forces are constantly fighting each other, so you are not free to carry out your good intentions"* (Galatians 5:16-17).

This statement of reality should awaken us to the battle and cause us to prepare for the conflict so we do not live our lives as victims of ignorance and weakness. The character of Christ is planted in us by the Spirit of God, who leads us into all understanding. Comprehending the conflict is the beginning of taking on His character.

The soul of the human being is shaped by either the flesh or the Spirit.

The soul of every human is the throne of self or the Savior, and the "throne room" is either led by the flesh or the person and character of Christ. The soul is the mind, the emotions and the will. It is the "brains" of the operation, ruled by the person, or by the person's god or God. Paul shares this reality in his letter to the church in Rome: *"Don't copy the behavior and customs of this world, but let God transform you into a new person by changing the way you think. Then you will learn to know God's will for you, which is good and pleasing and perfect"* (Romans 12:2).

PUTTING IT INTO PRACTICE

This explains some of the reasons why I was so confused while in Bolivia, and even for an extended period of time once I arrived home. God was communicating to me through my spirit, but my weak flesh was speaking a different message. The two were at odds, trying to influence my soul: the way I think, make decisions and feel. I found out later that I was also struggling with hypothyroid disease which can cause a low level of depression and fatigue not to mention weight gain! The flesh is emotional and affective, but there is hope if we are willing to accept the Father's plan.

Let me encourage you to allow the Spirit of God, seated on the inner throne of your soul, to cross-examine your senses, emotions, mind and desires. Before you make decisions, seek to understand what is influencing you. Is it what you see with your physical eyes, feel with your emotions, taste, or hear from the world? Is it correct biblical thinking? Is it what God is speaking to you?

Memorize Galatians 5:16-17 so that you will be constantly reminded of how to walk in the character of Christ.

POINTS TO PONDER

- Have you ever felt helpless or found yourself in a position that seemed hopeless? How did you deal with the situation?
- Where are you in your walk with the Holy Spirit? How has the Spirit helped you deal with the challenges of the "flesh"?
- Who currently resides on the "throne of your soul"? Where does your job, family, friends or activities fit in?

~ 26 ~
THE WAY YOU THINK

And now, dear brothers and sisters, one final thing. Fix
our thoughts on what is true, and honorable, and right, and
pure, and lovely, and admirable. Think about things that are
excellent and worthy of praise. Keep putting into practice all you
learned and received from me—everything you heard from me
and saw me doing. Then the God of peace will be with you.
– PHILIPPIANS 4:8-9

While I was a youngster, my uncle Jimmy was my pastor for several years. Sometimes after an evening service, I would stay at church and play with my cousin while my uncle would counsel or work in his study. On one particular night, as we were driving off, he stopped and asked me to run into the sanctuary to retrieve his Bible, which he had left on the pulpit.

My childish imagination ran wild! The church doors loomed large and castle-like as I turned the key and pulled with all my might to create enough space to squeeze my body into the dark lobby. I shivered when the door slammed shut behind me. As I made my way toward the inner doors of the sanctuary, I suddenly sensed many invisible and visible beings watching me and waiting to pounce on my little body.

Once inside, the moonlight illuminated the room just enough for my eyes to construct a basic outline of the pews and the massive pulpit. I was sure that many dark "things" were poised, waiting for an opportunity to grab me. I imagined one to be the devil himself. I could hear only two things: my heart racing fast and my lungs breathing. As I arrived at the pulpit, I searched with my hands and squinting eyes. Once my uncle's Bible was in my grasp, I ran out of the church as fast as I could!

Children have a vivid imagination in the dark. Their minds are very active because the environments and people in their lives seem so large. Adults imagine things in the dark too. But this is a different kind of darkness—it is spiritual.

While children see things "bigger than life," adults see *God* as "bigger than life." Often, we believe our problems are too trivial for His attention, or believe He simply is not that practical. This way of thinking is not a reflection of Christ's character.

CHRIST'S CHARACTER ALIVE IN YOUR MIND

Realize there is a right and wrong way to think.

Paul implies this when he instructs us to guide our thoughts toward proper things. He says, "*Fix your thoughts on what is true and honorable and right. Think about things that are pure and lovely and admirable. Think about things that are excellent and worthy of praise.* (Philippians 4:8).

Using broad examples, he teaches us to concentrate on the areas of truth, honor, righteousness, purity, love, admiration, a job well done, and qualities worthy of expressing praise and thanksgiving.

Is Paul suggesting that we live in denial and refuse to see the other side of life? Is he blind to the realities of death, sickness and sins against humanity and God? I don't think so. Instead, I believe he is offering at least three things when he asks us to choose to dwell on goodness.

First, it does no good to curse the darkness since the evil of this world is obvious to the Christian. The believer, however, is more interested in the activities of light, curious to see what the Lord is doing in spite of pain and sin. This is why the children of God are excited about how He is casting His brightness on the shadow of despair—and Spirit-filled believers desire to be part of God's activities. We enjoy being on the winning team!

Second, Paul is teaching us how to worship and enjoy the presence of God in our lives each moment of every day by noticing what He is doing.

Third, this kind of thought process influences others to view circumstances in the light of heaven. If we do this, we will not waste energy cursing the darkness. Rather, we will be busy noticing what God is doing and pointing it out to those who desire to see.

Thinking like Christ requires practice.

To become an expert at a task requires both instruction and experience. You can practice once in a while and notice little or no improvement, or you can make a commitment to repeat the task as often as it takes to experience deep change. Commitment is the repetitive process of doing what is right. Paul expresses: *"Keep putting into practice all you learned and received from me—everything you heard from me and saw me doing"* (Philippians 4:9).

We can do exactly what the apostle is recommending by becoming students of his books in the New Testament and by identifying and learning from the modern day "Pauls" in our lives. His writings teach us much concerning how God is making all things good.

There are people in your church who have proper thinking. Can you identify these individuals? If so, follow their example; if not, get busy and find them!

The experience of God's peace follows good thinking.

You can't become peaceful until you are filled with the presence of God—and it is impossible to be filled with His presence until you trade your way of thinking for His. When you do, the Father's peace always follows. As Paul writes, *"Then the peace of God will be with you"* (Philippians 4:9).

Peace is the clear benefit of proper thinking—which begins when we focus our thoughts on the Lord. When we dwell on Him we consider who He is, what He has done for us, and what our response should be. We focus on the fact He is working in our world and our lives, and that He transcends time and space. In other words, God is never trapped or confused by earthly events. His perfect plan will prevail. This kind of thinking is not only right; it brings peace to the soul.

PUTTING IT INTO PRACTICE

Take Paul's advice and act upon his wisdom. Grab your journal or get your laptop and do exactly what Paul says to do. Write down the things in your life that are based upon the truth—what is honorable and right. Jot down examples of purity, love and what you admire. Then thank God for these blessings. Begin to see the goodness and righteousness which is alive and well within you, even though you live in a corrupt, fallen world. If you concentrate on the good, it becomes a way of thinking, and a pattern for life.

POINTS TO PONDER

- What are the "dark" things that scare you now or have in the past?
- What is God using in your life today to train or mold you? Have you found contentment in the experience?
- How do you practice "right thinking"?

~27~
YOUR BODY

*Don't you realize that your body is the
temple of the Holy Spirit, who lives in you and was
given to you by God? You do not belong to yourself,
for God bought you with a high price. So you
must honor God with your body.*

– 1 CORINTHIANS 6:19-20

The first chapter of John's gospel teaches that Jesus Christ was God embodied in flesh and that He was 100% human and 100% God. This is difficult—if not impossible—to visualize. Nevertheless, the fact remains that Jesus' body was made of flesh and was subjected to our human need for nutrition, water, exercise, grooming and rest. For Christ to be God in the flesh indicates the Almighty must have a high regard for His creation of the human body, since He chose to appear in this form as He walked with the people of the first century.

Christians don't often talk about the body except in negative terms. In fact, the Bible seems to indicate much of our problems derive from the flesh. Many of the major "don'ts" of Scripture pertain to the body: including avoiding sexual relations outside of marriage and refusing to fill our bodies with too much wine, food, pleasure—and too much of anything.

The Bible also warns against, *"...the lust of the flesh, the lust of the eyes, and the pride of life"* (1 John 2:16 KJV).

Jesus said it would be better to remove any part of the body before allowing it to hurt another person, especially a child or a young believer.

Yet, Paul tells us we are the temple of the Holy Spirit. In biblical terms, our body is the place where God lives and should reign so that He

137

can be seen by others.

CHRIST'S CHARACTER IN YOUR BODY

Remember, God created people in His likeness.

The book of Genesis gives us a conversational sound bite within the community of the Creator: *"Then God said, 'Let us make human beings in our image, to be like us. They will reign over the fish in the sea, the birds in the sky, the livestock, all the wild animals on the earth, and the small animals that scurry along the ground.' So God created human beings in his own image. In the image of God he created them; male and female he created them. Then God blessed them and said, 'Be fruitful and multiply. Fill the earth and govern it. Reign over the fish in the sea, the birds in the sky, and all the animals that scurry along the ground'"* (Genesis 1:26-28).

You are made in the image of God. This does not mean He is an enormously sized, human-looking creature and we are small replicas of Him. But it does indicate He has given us the ability to reason, create, relate, choose, rule, etc. Although we are more than flesh and blood, our bodies are an invaluable part of our existence and assist us in the experiences and expressions of living.

God's original creation of the human body was free from all the flaws we struggle with today. As new creations in Christ, our body will ultimately die, but while we live, the presence of God in our soul allows us to discipline our physical beings for the Father's purposes. Our motivation for elevating respect for the body is not to create a fantasy of eternal life in this earthly shell, or seeking the mythical fountain of youth. It is, however, to consider the role of the body in Christian living.

To be like Christ, we are called to master our body.

The apostle Paul is a good example. He knew bodily discipline was important to his mission and understood how the appetites of "the physical" would eventually control his energy, health, moods, and the effectiveness of his ministry. Paul's letter to the Christians at Corinth included this conviction: *"I discipline my body like an athlete, training it to do what it should. Otherwise, I fear that after preaching to others I myself might be disqualified"* (1 Corinthians 9:27).

Our love for God compels us to step up to the challenge of healthy nutrition and regular exercise. Many of us find this part of the Christian life enjoyable, while others wish they could just write off sloppy living in God's accounting of grace. However you view this, taking care of ourselves is vital since it indicates our faithfulness to God.

Evaluating this area of Christ's character in me is not one of my favorite practices. As I have aged and no longer play team sports, I find physical training to be difficult because there seems to be no reason, no athletic challenge on the horizon. A couple of years ago while jogging, I questioned the relevance of this panting, sweating, and time-consuming endeavor. I was really struggling and asked, "Why am I doing this?"

By the grace of God, I was able to paraphrase Paul's words as an answer, "Because I desire to honor God in my body, making it my slave so that I can serve God here on earth as long and faithfully as I can."

Immediately, my attitude changed. I didn't break any time records, but I regained the emotional stamina needed to finish my race. I still wrestle with this subject from time to time, but the motive of honoring God by being more like Christ keeps me going. I hope this will be true for you as well.

Paul exhorts us further: *"Do not let any part of your body become an instrument of evil to serve sin. Instead, give yourselves completely to God, for you were dead, but now you have new life. So use your whole body as an instrument to do what is right for the glory of God"* (Romans 6:13).

PUTTING IT INTO PRACTICE

Evaluate the character of Christ in how you take care of your body. Most of us need to pay more attention to both exercise and nutrition. If you have tried to exert self-discipline in this area but have failed, welcome to the club! From one who has "been there, done that," let me offer some suggestions from personal experience.

If you are an individual who eats healthy and exercises five days a week, please be patient with the rest of us. As you read the following list, please remember that one small step leads to another. Your exercise will improve your eating habits and good eating habits will encourage you to exercise. So here we go:

1. Dedicate a journal just for the purpose of monitoring and mastering your body. Start by writing down a few thoughts on why you want to make changes. When your will is weak, read these notes because they will stimulate you to do the right things.

2. Keep a record of what you eat and drink, your exercise schedule, your goals, thoughts and progress.

3. Find a partner or a coach who will work with you. There are many outstanding exercise and nutritional programs available. Be patient with yourself, and don't look for excuses to quit. Most of us fail in our pursuit of perfection, so commit yourself to being consistent. Part of succeeding is becoming stronger through both failures and successes. A godly will is developed through toil; it does not arrive special delivery.

4. Listen to people who really care about you and follow this advice: Start slow, have fun, celebrate each success, confess failures, ask for help, don't spend a lot of money, avoid comparing yourself to others, and above all—don't quit!

POINTS TO PONDER

- What about your physical appearance would you change if you could?
- What are the appetites that fight to control your physical body? How are you doing in your struggle to overcome them?
- Which is the bigger obstacle: diet or exercise?
- List two people (other than a spouse) you can approach to encourage you and hold you accountable.

~ 28 ~
PURITY

*God's will is for you to be holy, so stay away from
all sexual sin. Then each of you will control his own
body and live in holiness and honor—not in lustful passion
like the pagans who do not know God and his ways. Never
harm or cheat a Christian brother in this matter by violating his
wife, for the Lord avenges all such sins, as we have solemnly
warned you before. God has called us to live holy lives, not
impure lives. Therefore, anyone who refuses to live by these
rules is not disobeying human teaching but is rejecting
God, who gives his Holy Spirit to you.*
– 1 THESSALONIANS 4:3-8

Few things carry the weight of shame like sexual sin. For many it is the ultimate test of self-control. As a former youth pastor, I worked with many young men and women who unfortunately experienced firsthand the scars of giving in to sexual temptation. As a pastor, the same could be said of marriages slaughtered in sacrifice to the god of adultery.

Many seem to think God is some type of kill-joy in demanding we abstain from sexual expressions outside of marriage. Those with this attitude have forgotten that while human beings are unfaithful, God can be trusted. We've all heard people justify their behavior with phrases such as, "He listens to me," or "We love each other." Yet we know that the majority of human beings move in and out of "love" because of an unquenchable quest for the perfect relationship.

The thirst for intimacy outside of God's design, will never be satisfied. First, because there are no perfect people there will be no perfect relationships, those without problems. Commitment to purity is birthed and practiced by believing that God's way of doing things is based upon His original plan. In other words, godly morality works because it was created for our benefit. Second, any belief system outside of God's blueprint simply does not work.

CHRIST'S CHARACTER IN PURITY

The apostle Paul in the above text answers the question of God's will for our lives by explaining the Father's overriding purpose, as well as one of the outcomes of this objective. Let's begin by considering the Lord's plan for you and me.

God's main desire for each of us is that we willingly belong to Him.

Paul says it is *"...God's will for you to be holy"* (1 Thessalonians 4:3). It should be encouraging that the Almighty has a will and desire for you; it is also a life-giving discovery. His will is for you to be *sanctified*—set apart just for Him and His purposes. God expresses it plainly: "Your life counts; you matter to Me."

We know what sanctification is because we have personally practiced it with the power God has delegated to us. Two simple illustrations will help us see this. Some women have saved, or set aside, one or two special dolls from their childhood. When I was a small boy, I collected baseball cards and throughout my life I set apart those that were most valuable to me. In some cases, my decision was based upon their financial value, but most often it was because of a sentimental attachment. The difference between you and your childhood possessions is that you have the ability to respond to your Owner.

What is your role in the sanctifying desire of God? Is it your willingness to give yourself wholly to the Lordship of Jesus Christ—not partially, but fully? As you allow Him to set you apart on a daily basis, you grow more like Him and discover His destiny for you. As He becomes your Lord, you gain a sense of belonging, ownership and purpose.

One of God's specific desires is for you to be sexually pure.

Paul explains. *"God has called us to live holy lives, not impure lives"* (1 Thessalonians 4:7).

The apostle spells out sexual purity by commanding we abstain from fornication. The original word he used was *porneias,* which is a broad term describing illicit sexual activity between a man and woman outside the boundary of marriage.

When you give yourself completely to the Lord, you have the desire to submit your will to His. When this happens, your fellowship with the Spirit of God produces the power to control your appetites and desires. Then, as your fellowship with the Lord governs your sexual desires, you not only honor God, but you esteem others by protecting their virginity, marriages and sexual purity.

As your sexuality is expressed within the boundary of marriage, you distinguish yourself from the lust-worshiping nature of the world. Those who bow to the gods of sexual pleasure outside of marriage walk in defiance of the Lord's design and standards. By practicing restraint, you experience sexuality as God intended and become a living example of sanctification.

As followers of Christ, this process is strengthened by identifying and defeating influences which corrupt and contaminate purity. During the 1970s and 1980s, the American church experienced a short-lived revival toward sexual virtue. The church identified sensual rock music as one of the main influences for impurity. Bonfires were organized for the purpose of burning thousands of record albums as believers gave up their old ways by throwing their once-precious collections into the fire. Some might consider this action legalistic, naive, over-the-top, or simply ridiculous. As a firsthand witness to some of these commitments to purity, I saw many lives change for the better. There is plenty of good music available in and outside of the church, but there are also influences which need to be removed from believers.

No one has ever claimed that living a chaste life would be easy. It comes by loving God and denying self-gratification—and is an ongoing commitment to identify and overrule the impurities of our flesh. Call it a commitment to virginity until marriage; call it second or even third virginity, or the rebirth of your marriage bed. Call it whatever best describes the specifics of your repentance, but do this in the strength of Jesus Christ.

Perhaps you think this call is a little too zealous and you may believe I have forgotten about the grace, forgiveness and understanding of a merciful God who identifies with our frailties. Let me remind you how Jesus dealt with the woman who was caught in adultery; the account is found in John Chapter 8. While a mob was ready to stone the guilty woman to death as a means of purification, Jesus was ready to cleanse something greater: the ongoing disease of sin.

The Lord did this by demonstrating that His grace and mercy, packaged in forgiveness, will equip the weakest soul to rejoice and enjoy a changed life. As the rock-clinching crowd dispersed after Jesus challenged those without sin to cast the first stone, He turned to the woman and spoke: "Your accusers have left, now go and sin no more." It's the last few words we often miss, "go and sin no more." This is the grace of Christ which empowers us to break the habitual pattern of sexual immorality, but His grace is not an excuse to keep on sinning.

Our conviction for purity comes from our inner fellowship with God.

Paul writes: *"Therefore, anyone who refuses to live by these rules is not disobeying human teaching but is rejecting God, who gives his Holy Spirit to you"* (1 Thessalonians 4:8).

Believers submit to the presence of Christ in their hearts. Their conviction to follow the Lord comes not from outside influences, but from the Holy Spirit. To distinguish between the world's thinking, your own thoughts and the mind of Christ, you must know and study the written ministry of God—the Bible. It is your spiritual hearing aid.

As you read the Scriptures, you will be able to distinguish the whisper of God from all other voices. The New Testament presents it this way: *"All Scripture is God-breathed and is useful for teaching, rebuking, correcting and training in righteousness, so that the man of God may be thoroughly equipped for every good work"* (2 Timothy 3:16-17 NIV).

The Lord considers your purity to be of the utmost importance, even if you do not. And God takes very seriously the defrauding of a brother or sister. Even if another person willingly participates in sexual activities outside of the marriage covenant, you are guilty of including them in your sin. Paul reminds us of this when he explains how the outcome of our trespass will harm or exploit a brother or sister.

The words of Psalm 119: 9-11 affirm the power of God's activity through the Scriptures: *"How can a young man keep his way pure? By living according to your word. I seek you with all my heart; do not let me stray from your commands. I have hidden your word in my heart that I might not sin against you"* (Psalms 119:9-11 NIV).

PUTTING IT INTO PRACTICE

God desires to provide you with an opportunity to set apart your sexual life for the first time, the second time, or whatever is true for you. Please take this opportunity to express your gratefulness to the Lord, who longs to bless your sexual life through purity. Embrace the fact that the strength for a sexually pure life stems from a close walk with the living Christ and His written Word.

Perhaps you are willing to share your commitment to purity with another believer in Christ. Consider the following prayer as a way to verbalize your willingness to follow Jesus in this way: *Lord, I give myself to You because I belong to You. I desire to live a life of sexual purity. Help me today and everyday to know and experience Your strength as I seek to fulfill Your plan for me.*

POINTS TO PONDER

■ Is your life sanctified by God? In what way is this demonstrated?

- Identify objects in your home that may cause you or a loved one to stumble in purity. What are you doing to safeguard against these temptations?
- Can you say you have accepted God's grace and "sinned no more," or have you used His grace as an excuse to continue sinning?

~ 29 ~
TEMPTATION

*No temptation has seized you except what
is common to man. And God is faithful; he will not
let you be tempted beyond what you can bear. But
when you are tempted, he will also provide a
way out so that you can stand up under it.*
— 1 CORINTHIANS 10:13 NIV

Some people can walk right by a chocolate store without even noticing. I need a small army to drag me away; otherwise I'm in the shop ordering a big piece of milk-chocolate-covered caramel!

Don't get me wrong, there's nothing harmful about a little candy every once in a while, but even a small pleasure like this can become habit-forming and potentially damaging to our bodies. Unfortunately, addictions rarely stay in their own backyard. Instead they tend to climb over fences and motivate gangs of bad practices. In other words, one small thing quickly leads to another.

Both you and I know this topic is much more serious than resisting chocolate. We all are tempted, but not always in the same way. No matter what your weakness, it's shared by multitudes of others! We can be enticed to misuse our thoughts and our words, or be lured by money, success or sex. Others are tempted to hide weaknesses and their true self. Still others are strangely pulled to steal, kill, or hurt another person. Let's face it, the possibilities for evil are endless.

Trials and difficulties birth a variety of problems, but we don't need tests to be tempted; we seem to easily find it on our own! To be guilty of weakness is to consider aborting the plans and will of the Father. In this sense, enticements create an awareness of options, either God's way or my way. If I say or think "I am being swayed," I am already admitting that if I make the wrong decision, it is not His choice. I have consciously chosen my own way.

CHRIST'S CHARACTER OVER TEMPTATION

When tempted, take time to understand your true need.

If something is appealing to you, it is because you believe it has the ability to satisfy one or more of your basic needs. And it is possible the lure, no matter how wrong, can provide some temporary satisfaction. The problem is, many sins are teasers that lead you into more destructive behavior.

Paul observes: *"No temptation has seized you except what is common to man"* (1 Corinthians 10:13). What is common? Our needs! The apostle is recognizing how our temptations reveal our innermost desires. For example, if I do not realize that possessions cannot satisfy my need for contentment, it could eventually lead me to financial and relational ruin. Often, a person has to experience such hardship in order to appreciate the simple things of life.

So here's the trick: identify what a temptation is telling you about yourself. Does it reveal what makes you feel important? Is it uncovering unhealthy ways you deal with stress? Is it exposing a lack of intimacy and purity with your spouse? Is it asking who you trust? Is it testing your patience? Once you can honestly answer these questions, you have unveiled your true need. Then you will be able to resist destructive ways which *pretend* to satisfy, and embrace the thoughts and behaviors that *will* be fulfilling.

Defeat temptation by understanding the consequences of wrong choices.

Pastor Andy Stanley in Atlanta talks about the three areas of consequences: family, future, and faith. When being tempted, ask yourself, "How will my choice impact my family?" Often we do not realize how our decisions affect other people, especially those we love and respect. Many adults carry childhood scars inflicted upon them from the actions of a person of trust. We need to recognize that our character and behavior have longer lives than our bodies.

Next, ask yourself, "How will my decision impact my future?" We can either lie to ourselves, or we can stop and recognize that sin has a way of working itself to the surface like a weed through blacktop. While we may be able to fake it for a time, the weed is still spreading its roots, growing on the inside. When it reaches the surface, the damage has already been done: first to you, then to your family and future.

Notice Paul's statement, *"And God is faithful; he will not let you be tempted beyond what you can bear"* (v.13). In other words, the Lord expects you to overcome temptation—every one of them can be defeated. This is a promise from God. Are you too frail or weak? Are you too naive? No! Your Heavenly Father will never allow anything into your life He has not provided the strength for you to face and overcome.

To defeat the enemy we must understand the purpose of temptations and trials.

Paul writes, *"But when you are tempted, he will also provide a way out so that you can stand up under it"* (v.13).

I like the phrasing "so that you can stand up under it." This reminds me of those power lifters who squat down to pick up a barbell with hundreds of pounds of weight. The bar bends as the athlete proceeds to stand up. Then at the end of the lift, he throws the weight on the floor in front of him. Next, the weight lifter raises his arms in victory!

Does God give you more weight than you can lift? He promises, "No." Do you believe Him?

The purpose of temptation is for you to learn that God can be trusted; His way is always best.

So what does success look like when encountering temptation? Is it to see how much you can tempt yourself without weakening or giving in? Of course, not. It is to understand your true need, consider the consequences of the dark side, to see the path of escape and choose it! In doing so, you will grow stronger in your trust for God and your needs will continually be met.

PUTTING IT INTO PRACTICE

Be honest about your temptations by identifying some longer-term issues that seem to constantly torment you. Beneath each one, write down what true need is being uncovered: Next note some weakness which tends to "pop up" from time-to-time and then consider what this may be revealing.

Memorize 1 Corinthians 10:13.

POINTS TO PONDER

- As a Christ-follower, how has your view of temptation changed? Have you found fighting it to be easier? If so, how?
- Share a past experience where giving into the lure of the world affected your faith, future, or family.
- Name two people you can call for reliable support when going through temptations.

~ 30 ~
HUSBANDS

For husbands, this means love your wives,
just as Christ loved the church...
– EPHESIANS 5:25

When I think about the role of a husband, I automatically revisit my childhood. It may seem odd, but when the subject "husband" is raised, I go back home in my mind and begin to think of my mother. My boyhood thoughts concerning her are not much different than those I hold today. She is a simple woman of faith—a hard worker and fiercely loyal to her family. I always believed my mom was the best looking lady in town. She is a wonderful cook and homemaker, and I am still amazed at how she can take any house and turn it into a home. My mom nurtured her kids and respected her husband, so it was never difficult for me to love her. She was, and is, all heart; giving everything to her family.

A wife is a gift to a man. She may or may not bear children, but she helps her husband discover masculinity as God intended. Some may be offended by the idea a woman is "a gift" to her spouse because they will interpret the phrase in such a way it reduces her to that of a possession. But this is not what the phrase implies. Instead, it means men and women who are called to marriage were made by the Creator to complete one another and reveal a reflection of God through their relationship.

Let me be more candid. Can you imagine a world populated by men only? No thank you! Some are hypersensitive when it comes to the generalizations made between men and women. They look for an untruth as they pour over every word or listen to each phrase. I suppose this can go so far as to even deny the obvious biological differences between male and female. Therefore, when we make generalizations we are simply recognizing some things are more typical of one gender than the other. Whatever these differences may be, they are more dictated by God's design than by the influence of environments, experiences or personalities.

CHRIST'S CHARACTER IN THE HUSBAND

He loves her.

One word sums up the husband's responsibility – love. As Paul tells men, *"And you husbands must love your wives with the same love Christ showed the church"* (Ephesians 5:25).

Loving your wife centers on devoting your attention, time and self to her. It is not about trying to change her, making her the woman you want her to be. Also, it's not creating her into the image of your mom—or perhaps the mother you never had. It's just loving her.

The apostle Paul uses the Greek verb *agapao* to describe the specific type of love a husband is to have for his wife. This kind of affection is completely selfless. It comes from God and you bestow it on your wife as a loving response to your Heavenly Father's love for you. The parallel between a husband's love for his wife and Christ's love for His church is realized when we recognize that the Greek word for the church (*ekklesia*) is feminine.

The strength and selflessness of this adoration can be held in contrast to two other types of love expressed in the Bible through the Greek language. Pay attention to the fact that Paul did not use the word *eros* (sexual passion) nor did he use the word *philia* (family affection) to describe the love a man must give to his wife. Though both of these can and should be present in a marriage, neither provides God's ideal for the foundation of a blessed union. Instead, Paul uses the same word for love which describes the adoration Jesus Christ has for His church, which is fully devoted and selfless.

To love your wife is to set her apart from all others.

Scripture tells us Christ, *"...gave up his life for her to make her holy and clean, washed by the cleansing of God's word"* (Ephesians 5:25-26).

To "make her holy" or blameless is to sanctify her by the predetermined resolve of your love. This means to set her apart from all other human relationships. In doing so, she becomes a unique recipient of God's grace being delivered through you. By making her your most important human relationship, your wife receives from God whatever she needs to become all He intends for her to be.

Though you will include others in your realm of godly affection, your wife must never become subordinate to anyone. She is your most cherished human relationship. An old Jewish wedding custom has the bridegroom say to the bride, "Behold thou art sanctified to me." This tradition was a public confession of a spiritual truth and a vow of human intention. Additionally, it implies and supports the idea that the bond of marriage superintended by God's presence will not decay to such levels as polygamy, adultery or divorce.

To love your wife is to nurture her as you would your own body.

The healthy husband takes care of himself so that he can love his wife and honor God in all he does. The Bible teaches, *"...husbands ought to love their wives as they love their own bodies. For a man who loves his wife actually shows love for himself"* (Ephesians 5:28).

To some this might seem like double talk, but it is spiritually sound, because in marriage two people become one. *"'At last!' the man exclaimed. 'This one is bone from my bone, and flesh from my flesh! She will be called "woman," because she was taken from "man."' This explains why a man leaves his father and mother and is joined to his wife, and the two are united into one"* (Genesis 2:23-24).

Therefore, to love your wife is to love the one body that is made up of both you and your wife. This is God's perfect design.

One of the most common temptations a husband has is to be harsh with his spouse. It is generally true that those who possess physical dominance can resort to behavior which resembles the playground bully. A godly husband, however, will not use such tactics when tension arises. He will see his wife as God's creation and one who needs to feel safe in his presence no matter what the circumstances. This sense of safety, respect and honor is damaged when the husband raises his voice in anger—not to mention any kind of physical abuse. Paul writes: *"Husbands, love your wives and never treat them harshly"* (Colossians 3:19).

PUTTING IT INTO PRACTICE

Make your wife your most important human relationship. Regardless of the condition of your marriage, loving her as Christ loves the church will transform your bond and bring honor and glory to God. Those who know you and see your healthy marriage will wonder what created such a positive change. This will become a wonderful opportunity to demonstrate how the Lord is still working in the lives of people today. As we read His Word and obey it with joy-filled hearts, God changes things.

This week memorize Ephesians 5:25. When you sense you are struggling in your marriage, pray these same words back to God. He will guide you into all truth and you will gain the love and perspective you need to love your wife with unconditional *agape* love.

POINTS TO PONDER

- What was the relationship like with your father and mother? How has this affected your marriage or relationships?
- What keeps you from acting toward your wife in the way Paul has instructed? What can you do to change?
- Can you ask your wife out on a "date night" and make her feel loved? When was the last time you sent a card or flowers to your wife?

~ 31 ~
WIVES

...submit to one another out of reverence for Christ. For wives, this means submit to your husbands as to the Lord.
— EPHESIANS 5:21-22

"Behind every good man is a good woman." We've all heard this phrase. Is it true?

Let's start by examining the word "behind." Is a good wife behind her husband, beside her husband, or in front of him? Perhaps all three at different times, in a variety of ways, and based upon certain circumstances.

Nevertheless, the word "behind" was placed in this cliché for a reason. It has long been assumed that a good man provides a honored place for a woman to stand, live, grow, laugh, and to cry. But the saying is meant to emphasize the goodness of a woman, and part of this is the willingness to support her husband. So the finer qualities of a woman creates opportunities for a man. In fact, every husband makes greater strides when he senses the unconditional love and support of those around him, especially his wife.

A man is a unique creation of God, just as complex as God's creation of a woman. He has physical strength. Sometimes we ask, "He is strong on the outside, but is he as strong on the inside?" So what does it mean for a man to have inner strength? And how does a husband become worthy of being known as "a good man?"

Believe it or not, a wife plays a pivotal role in the growth and inner strength of her husband by allowing Christ to live through her.

CHRIST'S CHARACTER AT WORK IN THE WIFE

Love your husband by submitting to him.

A Christian woman yields to her husband out of reverence for God's design and to invite leadership. The whole structure of society ordered by God is one of mutual submission: godlike cooperation. Christians are called to defer themselves to civil authorities, to church leaders and to parents. Those in authority are called by God to yield themselves to the virtues of goodness and service.

The apostle Paul compares the submission of a wife to her husband to that of the church to Jesus Christ. *"For a husband is the head of his wife as Christ is the head of the church. He is the Savior of his body, the church. As the church submits to Christ, so you wives should submit to your husbands in everything"* (Ephesians 5:23-24).

As Christ is the head of the earthly church, so the husband is head of the wife. Yes, the wife has but one Savior, who is Jesus Christ, but the husband plays a similar role of submission by giving his life for her by loving, nourishing and protecting.

God's gift and practice of this in human relationships cultivates genuine love and respect for one another. When a husband receives his role as head of the wife in humility, his attitude encourages the same from her. And when the wife willingly and voluntarily submits herself to her husband, she humbles his inner man. This causes him to seek greater character and love from God so he does not disappoint those he loves. The hierarchy of human relationships and institutions were never designed to overwhelm the most divine principle of all: mutual submission and service.

Paul explains this in broader terms that can be applied in every possible human context: *"Because of the privilege and authority God has given me, I give each of you this warning: Don't think you are better than you really are. Be honest in your evaluation of yourselves, measuring yourselves by the faith God has given us. Just as our bodies have many parts and each part has a special function, so it is with Christ's body. We are many parts of one body, and we all belong to each other"* (Romans 12:3-5).

Paul's advice for a wife to yield herself to her husband is contained within the context of marriage and in no way suggests that women in general are to be subject to men, nor does it imply women are inferior to men. However, loving submission is the way a wife has been designed by God to love her husband. Her yielding allows him the opportunity to grow in his ability to love God by loving his wife the way Christ loves the church, which is by giving His life for her.

Love your husband by demonstrating respect for him.

The counsel of Paul for the wife to respect her husband exposes his need for esteem and honor: *"...and the wife must respect her husband"* (Ephesians 5:33). The man should be revered as he learns to follow Christ's model of love for the church. He will need a longsuffering wife as he discovers through experience and spiritual growth what loving her this way actually looks like.

It is dangerous for a woman to allow herself to lose respect for her husband through the years as he struggles to discover how to love and lead his wife the way Christ would. After all, Jesus is a tough act to follow!

In addition, the Scriptures assume the husband is living in such a manner *worthy* of respect. If he fails in the ideal virtues of marriage, the wife will be tempted to pull back from her commitment to submit and to respect. But if she gives into such urges, she will be guilty of perpetuating the problem by creating a competition of wills within the relationship.

PUTTING IT INTO PRACTICE

The seven godly disciplines listed below will help every wife continue to respect her husband during the growing years:

1. Demonstrating submission and respect for your husband demonstrates your love for Christ.
2. Honestly examine your attitude of cooperation and grace.
3. Remember that your job is to love your husband and God's work

is to change him for the better. When you try to transform him, you're actually getting in God's way.

4. Compare how willingly you forgive your husband with how willingly Christ forgave you.

5. Pray for your husband and thank God for him, instead of grading him in his performance.

6. Express to your spouse what you appreciate about him, in the past and the present.

7. Learn things you can do to support him and realize he needs encouragement just as you do.

If you are a mother as well as a wife, the best gift you can present to your child or children is to work in partnership with God and your husband to create the finest marriage possible. Most attempted parenting skills will pale in the presence of a great marriage. In fact, good parenting flows *out* of a good marriage—where two imperfect people submit themselves to the Lordship of Jesus Christ and to one another.

Regardless of your initial thoughts and emotions concerning the roles of marriage, I urge you to consider this one truth: God is the creator and designer of earthly unions. He knows how to make them work. If both husband and wife trust His word, a healthy marriage will result. If you are the only one who is following in the ways of Christ, do not be discouraged because you and God make a majority. Trust and see what the Lord can do.

POINTS TO PONDER

- What was your relationship with your father like growing up? Do you think this has affected how you relate to your husband?
- How is the world's interpretation of submission different from what Paul talks about?
- How do you show respect to your husband or boyfriend? How can you improve?

~ 32 ~
YOUR WORK

*Slaves, obey your earthly masters in everything
you do. Try to please them all the time, not just
when they are watching you. Serve them sincerely
because of your reverent fear of the Lord. Work willingly
at whatever you do, as though you were working for the
Lord rather than for people. Remember that the Lord
will give you an inheritance as your reward, and
that the Master you are serving is Christ.*

– COLOSSIANS 3:22-24

Not every type of labor is enjoyable, but most people like their work and the ability to see accomplishment. It's the way God designed us. While some like to work with their hands, others would rather deal with ideas and concepts. Some prefer to work alone while others thrive on the team concept.

Let's get personal. You may not be satisfied with your current employment. It could be because you do not see any *significance* in your assignment. Your dissatisfaction could also be driven by the fact you simply do not relish the *type* of activity in which you are engaged. Perhaps you feel you are better suited for a different position. Of course there is another factor: You may dislike the people you work beside or the ones who employ you.

What about those who are full-time students? Is learning and preparing for the future considered work? What about stay-at-home parents? Does such activity qualify as important, or simply necessary? There are still more possibilities. What if you cannot work due to physical disabilities? What if you are retired? What if you are financially independent? And finally, how should Christ's character be magnified in the work-life of one of His followers?

CHRIST'S CHARACTER IN THE WORKPLACE

See the bigger picture.

Many years ago, one of my associates shared with me and several others his view of God's strategy to change the world. In my own words, this is how he described the Lord's plan of action: "God's view of significance is often different than ours. At times we judge success based upon titles, salaries, fame and power. But that's not God's perspective. He recognizes that spiritually lost people occupy every realm of the human existence. Some are rich, while others are poor. Some are born sick and others live 100 years. What God does by His mercy, grace and omniscience is to place believers in every sector of life so there is a God-loving, Christ-serving witness near every dark corner in this sinful world. At times the Father reaches out and touches a humble farm boy and calls him to speak to the nations, like Billy Graham! Then He places men and women in political offices around the world. He appoints spiritual leaders over specific countries and states. But this is not sufficient, so He draws pastors to local churches. He then calls executives, software engineers, school teachers, county and city workers, clerks, and many others and places them strategically so that more people can be influenced by the presence of God's Spirit living in His children. He speaks to stay-at-home parents for the purpose of influencing their children and those in their neighborhood, church and school. No believer is left out of God's amazing plan to change the world!"

The first time I heard this view of the Father's activity it encouraged me to rethink the idea of personal significance. In this sense, God assigns the believer a location and a job, and thus a circle of influence. Every Christian has a practical role to play in the Kingdom. It is our choice to accept or reject it.

To see our workplace as an opportunity to glorify God is to demonstrate reverence for Him as Colossians 3:22 suggests. Whether we are digging ditches, cleaning restrooms, trading stocks or making high-powered decisions, a believer can turn those around him or her toward God. We need to see the larger picture, which also includes an eternal reward for working with a healthy attitude and being thankful for the platform to make a difference, no matter how difficult it might seem.

Set an example for others to follow.

Christ's character in you wants to model what it means to be greater than the small, irritating circumstances which accompany the workplace. While many strive for recognition and jockey for position, the character of Christ chooses to do the things other people would rather forget. Helping another person become successful instead of making sure everyone knows about your abilities is something Christ would do—as is being willing to do more and expect less.

I have heard this attitude called the "and then some" performance. In other words, the character of Christ does what is expected "and then some" more. Why? Because it's in God's nature to redeem, restore and lift up a place with His goodness so people might seek Him.

How many days go by without an honest and sincere acknowledgment of the Lord's goodness and mercies? You can keep a positive outlook on the job by remembering one thing: Ultimately, your work is for God—regardless of who signs your paycheck.

Trust in God for your current work struggles and your future.

People who perform their duties with a good disposition are paid and promoted more than people who make minimal effort. Are there exceptions? In the short-term, yes; in the long-term, never. Even if you are not recompensed on earth, you will be rewarded eternally! Research reveals people who advance are those who get along with others and demonstrate positive teamwork and integrity.

When you are tempted to take short cuts—lying, stealing, self-promoting and compromising—stop and remember Who you truly work for and Who really is making the decisions. The wheels of justice and righteousness turn very slowly for those who expect everything to work out here on earth. Your career may begin on earth, yet it does not end here. God can be trusted to make all things right in His time. Work for your Heavenly Father, not for temporary rewards.

PUTTING IT INTO PRACTICE

As you begin each workweek, take God with you by remembering what Christ wants to do in and through you at your place of employment, whether this is at home, the construction site, the office, the school or in the marketplace. Start each morning with the following prayerful thoughts: Thank God for your work assignment. Ask the Lord to flow through you in your endeavors. Ask Him to reveal the significance of your contribution. Remind yourself that your real employer is the Creator of all things. Finally, confess to the Lord that you trust Him in this job and for your future.

POINTS TO PONDER

- Do you consider your work to be a burden or an opportunity? When were you happiest in your career?
- Can you identify the reason God has you in your current position? Have you asked Him to reveal His purpose for you? What is it?
- Describe your attitude toward your job? Are you displaying the glory of God?

~ 33 ~
MONEY

*Don't store up treasures here on earth, where
moths eat them and rust destroys them, and where
thieves break in and steal. Store your treasures in heaven,
where moths and rust cannot destroy, and thieves do
not break in and steal. Wherever your treasure is,
there the desires of your heart will also be.*

– MATTHEW 6:19-21

I enjoyed the year of training I received as a management intern during my seven-year employment at a well-known bank based in California. Some of the most interesting instruction was a week-long study of criminal schemes, including counterfeiting, fraud and bank robbers.

For a young man, this was really fascinating stuff because it reminded me of those "good guy/bad guy" movies I watched growing up. Through the training, I was exposed to a recent history of bank crimes, some of which resulted in death to innocent people. As I reflected on these facts, my boyhood fantasies were sobered by what certain people are capable of doing for the sake of money.

That same week my pastor preached a message on the subject of finances. More specifically, he spoke about the Father's giving nature and the new nature of God's people. Then he quoted an Old Testament prophet by the name of Malachi. He read the following words from the New American Standard Bible: *"Will a man rob God? Yet you are robbing Me! But you say, 'How have we robbed You?' In tithes and offerings. You are cursed with a curse, for you are robbing Me, the whole nation of you! Bring the whole tithe into the storehouse, so that there may be food in My house, and test Me now in this,"* says the Lord of hosts, *"if I will not open for you the windows of heaven and pour out for you a blessing until it overflows"* (Malachi 3:8-10 NASB).

163

Criminals were fresh on my mind. And according to this prophet, I was one of them. Now I had to make a decision concerning how I was going to deal with this "thing" called money.

THE CHARACTER OF CHRIST IS SEEN IN HOW WE VIEW MONEY

I own nothing; God owns everything.

Psalm 24:1 tells us that the earth is the Lord's, and everything in it This means I belong to God, plus my house, my abilities, my family, my friends, my church, and yes, even my money belongs to Him.

God has entrusted all of this and more to me so I can share with Him the joy of building His goodness on earth and distributing His resources where He directs. Since my family and I belong to Him, He desires some of His abundance be used to care for our welfare too! However, I don't need to try and fit as much into my life as possible before I die, because although I will pass from this earth, I will also live forever. To reword an old saying, "He who has the most toys does *not* win!" There is much more life ahead in eternity than there is in the here and now.

Jesus reminds us how uncertain is the wealth on this earth when He declares, *"Don't store up treasures here on earth, where moths eat them and rust destroys them, and where thieves break in and steal"* (Matthew 6:19).

All we spend our hard-earned cash on eventually grows old, becomes outdated and needs to be replaced. The more you make, the more you spend—and the more wealth you acquire, the more people there are who want a share of your good fortune. Here's the truth. Most of the war regarding money is won or lost in the battle for perspective. If you really think your income and your assets belong to you, you're in for a big surprise. Generally speaking, we experience stress and relational strife when we believe the funds in our possession are ours to use as we please, without considering the Lord's commands. But if you truly believe God owns it all, you have Someone to turn to for guidance. You will also understand greater purpose and meaning and enjoy the opportunity to participate with God in His work.

I look most like Christ when I give.

In my opinion, God is best described to the human mind as "generous." Before time began, He decided to create life in various forms. You and I represent God's generosity. He not only gave us a body, but also breath and an environment where we can experience His presence. Like Him, we can make decisions, create, forgive, relate and receive the many blessings of life. Among many other attributes, God is a giver.

To be like Christ in character involves giving back the resources the Father has entrusted to us: our emotions, time, energy, blessings, wisdom and our financial resources. But since there is no universal law or spiritual tax, we can give as much or as little as we want. There is no mandate which can be reduced down to a mathematical equation. However, there is a spiritual principle dating back to the earliest records of God's relationship with mankind.

The precedent set since the time of the original family was to offer sacrifices and tithes (one-tenth) to God (Genesis 3:21, 4:2-5, 14:20). These gifts are meant to promote the ultimate acknowledgment that we owe all we have and all we are to our God and Creator. In doing this we also contribute to the involvement and promotion of this Good News: Mankind has a point of origin and hope in this amazing Being we have learned to call God.

The principle of giving has little to do with just "doing your part." It's not about equal giving; it's more about equal sacrifice. It has less to do with the size of your bank account or your income than the attitude and practice of giving. Paul describes this principle: *"Whoever sows sparingly will also reap sparingly, and whoever sows generously will also reap generously. Each man should give what he has decided in his heart to give, not reluctantly or under compulsion, for God loves a cheerful giver"* (2 Corinthians 9:6-7 NIV).

This precept causes each of us to evaluate what "sparingly" means and what "generously" means. It is not a religious pie-in-the-sky idea, rather it is very practical. Paul says earlier: *"Give in proportion to what you have. Whatever you give is acceptable if you give it eagerly. And give according to what you have, not what you don't have. Of course, I don't mean your giving should make life easy for others and hard for yourselves. I only mean that there should be some equality"* (2 Corinthians 8:11-13).

To put it bluntly, giving generously is the Christian's normal mode of operation because this is what God does.

Invest in eternity.

In today's employment terminology we often hear the phrase "salary package," which refers to what the employer is providing in addition to one's take home pay. This might include vacation time, health benefits, retirement plans, bonuses and other creative ideas. The Bible teaches that Christians will be "joint heirs" with Christ in eternity. We will own in common what the Lord owns, and will be rewarded for how we contribute to the Kingdom for Christ's sake. In other words, our salvation package includes eternal rewards on top of our residence with Christ in heaven.

Our hearts always follow where we put God's money. This is another reason why giving to His work is important—it turns our hearts away from the temporary and toward the eternal. It is what Jesus means when He says, *"Store your treasures in heaven, where moths and rust cannot destroy, and thieves do not break in and steal. Wherever your treasure is, there the desires of your heart will also be"* (Matthew 6:20-21).

Eternal investments do not fade, they grow!

PUTTING IT INTO PRACTICE

It's difficult to argue against the precedent of giving ten percent of our income to the ministry of Jesus Christ through the local church. It's also hard to conclude this is all which is required of the believer. In light of these two factors, I encourage you to establish these new habits: Starting today, view everything in your possession as God's and seek Him for direction. Evaluate and set annual goals for giving. Do not let either your hardships or your wealth keep you from the joy of investing in eternity!

POINTS TO PONDER

- Do you view God as a giver or a taker? Why do you think He wants you to tithe?
- Why are we instructed to give to the church with our tithes and offerings? Do you have a goal for sacrificial giving?
- Do you cheerfully tithe? Why do you think some people struggle with giving?

~ 34 ~
SUFFERING

*We can rejoice, too, when we run into problems
and trials, for we know that they help us develop
endurance. And endurance develops strength of character,
and character strengthens our confident hope of salvation.
And this hope will not lead to disappointment. For we
know how dearly God loves us, because he has given
us the Holy Spirit to fill our hearts with his love.*

— ROMANS 5:3-5

The longer we are on this earth the more acquainted we become with suffering. Sometimes we experience pain, loss or injury for the mistakes we have made, while on other occasions it seems there is no apparent reason.

With the assistance of orbiting satellites, we are able to see events around the globe in real-time. In this sense, the world has become smaller and we are now more aware of tragedies as they occur in any nation.

Pain can be felt in many forms. It is physical, mental, emotional, even spiritual—and it seems no one is exempt. It may strike you or someone you know or dearly love. The effect can be acute or chronic. Suffering is experienced by newborns, the aged and everyone in between. How acquainted are you with heartache and anguish?

I do not consider myself a person who has absorbed many hurts in life, yet I can say I know pain. Let me give you a brief list. Compared to the average man, I am considered short—about 5' 6", and as a boy, I was poked fun of because of my height. I have suffered several painful physical injuries from athletics, some requiring extensive surgery. I watched my father weep as he mourned the death of my grandpa. Our first child died in my wife's womb late in the pregnancy. I saw one of my best friends die a painful and slow death at the age of 43. My youngest brother's battle with drugs has caused great pain to all of my family, especially my mom. Like many, I have been deeply hurt by failed relationships. I have stood beside people in ministry who are traveling through valleys of deep tragedy. Perhaps the greatest suffering comes from recounting all my sins, but I have learned that nothing good comes from this.

As my brief list indicates, I am probably no more acquainted with pain than the average person. And perhaps you recounted the suffering in your own life as you read through the last paragraph. Most of us know living can be rather hard, and we may be tempted to ask, "Why?" But the better question might be, "Is there a good side to suffering?" and "How does the presence of Christ make a difference?"

CHRIST'S PRESENCE IN SUFFERING

Suffering makes us more like Christ.

This statement is true because pain or distress causes us to become *enduring* people. Sure, it's much easier to be full of joy when things are going well, but to be joyful in the midst of trial and tribulation is a godly characteristic. Paul writes: *"We can rejoice, too, when we run into problems and trials, for we know that they help us develop endurance"* (Romans 5:3).

The character of Christ in us has distinctive qualities. One such attribute is that of endurance—a divine patience which, in the midst of pain, does not lose sight of God's goodness and His ultimate faithfulness. Though suffering may last a lifetime, it cannot compare to the eternal beauty God has promised to all His children. But it's not these promises which ultimately allow us to survive hardships; it is God Himself who gives us strength. It's the character of God in Christ which fortifies us.

Suffering makes us choose.

It has been said that our true colors are revealed in difficult times. These may be our deepest convictions, and on any given day we might tell others we trust God, no matter what circumstances may come our way. We might even *believe* it, yet it is not proven until it is tested by trial.

Also, we may profess we should always forgive when we have been wronged. This is easy to say because Jesus said it, yet it is more difficult to live out when you are emotionally wounded. It's times like these that force us to choose whether we will do what Christ's presence in us desires or to simply revert to our own methods. Paul writes: *"And endurance develops strength of character, and character strengthens our confident hope of salvation"* (Romans 5:4).

Another way to think of endurance is to remember that it is the opposite of quitting. If we throw in the towel, we have little patience with God. But if we continue in the way of Christ while walking through the valley of suffering, the character of Christ empowers us and becomes grafted into our very being. We become strong in the hope of our salvation.

Suffering draws us closer.

We often think of salvation as an escape from damnation, and sometimes view it as a destination called heaven. But salvation is much more than this; it is God Himself. While in the grip of anguish, our hope is not merely that the pain and hurt will end, but that we are fully known, loved and accepted by God in spite of the suffering. And it is possible to have sweet fellowship with Him in the midst of human trauma. This communion becomes dearer to us than the ending of pain.

Our inner wounds can take us places we otherwise might not have the courage to visit. But the endurance of Christ within us is transforming, causing our lives to express the divine presence of God's unfailing love. Paul writes: *"...this hope will not lead to disappointment. For we know how dearly God loves us, because he has given us the Holy Spirit to fill our hearts with his love"* (Romans 5:5).

PUTTING IT INTO PRACTICE

Take time to study the troubles of great men and women by reading about their lives. You will be astonished to know how God used suffering to help them reflect Jesus. And the more we are like God's Son, the more we know the Father. And as we understand Him, the better we become in enduring the trials of life.

Write down the choices you have regarding an issue you may be facing. List what you think the character of Christ would have you do on one side, then list your temptation in the next column. Once you have completed this, consider the rewards of enduring while contemplating the consequences of quitting. Notice an example below:

My current crisis: My child is in constant trouble at school and sometimes with the law.

The Enduring Character of Christ	My Temptations
Pray for my child	Scream at my child
Let my child reap the consequences	Rescue my child by blaming others
Discipline my child	Give up on my child
Trust God for the future	Stop praying

All suffering and anguish provides an opportunity for growth and greater hope in Jesus Christ. It also has caused many to give up the fight. The choice is truly ours to make.

POINTS TO PONDER

- Have you recently or are you now going through a difficult time? How will your relationship with Jesus affect the outcome?
- How has being a follower of Christ changed your perspective on suffering? Do you welcome it as part of God's plan for you?
- Has the pain of your past been used for God's glory? If so, how?

~ 35 ~
PERSECUTION

*But you, Timothy, certainly know what I teach,
and how I live, and what my purpose in life is. You know
my faith, my patience, my love, and my endurance. You know
how much persecution and suffering I have endured. You
know all about how I was persecuted in Antioch, Iconium,
and Lystra—but the Lord rescued me from all of it.
Yes, and everyone who wants to live a godly life
in Christ Jesus will suffer persecution.*

– 2 TIMOTHY 3:10-12

I've heard it said that more Christians are suffering in the face of persecution now than ever before in the history of Christianity. There are believers living in countries around the globe who know firsthand how real religious oppression is and how brutal it can become. Persecution, like anything else, comes in varying degrees.

As Americans, we have the opportunity to suffer for our faith even though we live in a country which boasts of religious freedom. As Paul told Timothy in the Scripture above, if you desire to live a godly life (and actually do), the chances are good you will experience some level of opposition.

Let's face it, certain believers may *deserve* to be persecuted due to the way they wave their so-called faith arrogantly and rudely in the face of those who do not believe. There are even Christians who torment other believers with their words and actions because of doctrinal or philosophical differences. It's an obvious statement but it needs to be said: We live in an angry world. Unfortunately, this is not just a problem with those who are opposed to Christ.

It's ironic to me that both Christians and non-Christians exhibit hostility toward God and against one another. Even though Christ came into the world to bear the sin, shame, hate and destitution of mankind, we still possess the ability to hurt each other. But it is in this very arena we discover the secret of being like Christ.

CHRIST IN PERSECUTION

Remember our poverty.

Never allow opposition to bully you or make you fall away from Jesus and His people. Christ warns us that those who backslide due to being targeted have no depth of faith: *"But since he has no root, he lasts only a short time. When trouble or persecution comes because of the word, he quickly falls away"* (Matthew 13:21 NIV).

Instead, let persecution remind you of mankind's poverty. Perhaps you are excluded from certain social circles because your faith is known. Maybe your family members mock you or, because of your commitment to Jesus Christ, you are discriminated against at work. In such moments it is appropriate to mourn the human condition—but at the same time be thankful that Christ has the opportunity to rule each heart.

When we grieve, we remember what we have lost. This is necessary in order to embrace what we have gained in Jesus, which is complete acceptance. As we see people rejecting the Lord and others, it should cause us to ask: Why did God's grace embrace me even though I am as unworthy of it as the next person? Though we may never be able to answer this question, asking it transforms our attitude toward God and others.

The reason we can love our enemies and treat them well is because our security is found in the character and person of Christ, who is active within us. This is why the persecuted believer knows no limit for love.

There are numerous accounts of Christ-filled men and women dying at the hands of angry people. In many of these cases, no malice or hate was displayed by these committed Christians as they were being martyred.

Remember the price that was paid.

Let persecution remind you of the indescribable love of God. Peter writes: *"For you know that God paid a ransom to save you from the empty life you inherited from your ancestors. And the ransom he paid was not mere gold or silver. It was the precious blood of Christ, the sinless, spotless Lamb of God. God chose him as your ransom long before the world began, but he has now revealed him to you in these last days"* (1 Peter 1:18-20).

He did this for you. When we encounter unwelcome harassment, we are educated as to the "why" of God's radical action in the death of Jesus on that bloodied cross one Friday afternoon. It was necessary if any legitimate offer of redemption could be made to those held in the grasp of great darkness.

When facing persecution, give thanks to God that He would count you worthy to feel just a little (not even a fraction) of the pain Jesus experienced. Peter describes the difference between suffering for wrongdoing and being persecuted for righteousness:

"Of course, you get no credit for being patient if you are beaten for doing wrong. But if you suffer for doing good and endure it patiently, God is pleased with you. For God called you to do good, even if it means suffering, just as Christ suffered for you. He is your example, and you must follow in his steps. He never sinned, nor ever deceived anyone. He did not retaliate when he was insulted, nor threaten revenge when he suffered. He left his case in the hands of God, who always judges fairly" (1 Peter 2:20-23).

Look ahead to the joy that awaits.

Persecution for Christ's sake plays a unique role in eternity. The Crown of Life will be given to all those who suffer for the Lord, yet never lose their trust. Jesus said, *"...remain faithful even when facing death,* [and] *I will give you the crown of life"* (Revelation 2:10).

It makes sense: the greater the battle, the greater the victory. Life often feels like a war zone—and to exhibit godly behavior does not necessarily make life easier. In fact, mirroring Jesus can add an extra dimension of difficulty. Yet, this is a Christian's calling, and Christ modeled the type of faithfulness which should inspire every authentic believer.

PUTTING IT INTO PRACTICE

Determine in prayer today to love and bless those who persecute you. Become a real and radical reflection of Jesus by allowing His character to live in and through you. Read 1 Peter and 2 Peter and re-read these every time you encounter opposition. Memorize 1 Peter 3:15.

POINTS TO PONDER

- Have you ever had to defend a position you knew to be right? Give an example. Were you tempted to back down?
- Have you had to defend your faith at work or in public? If not, can you say that you've challenged yourself to tell the "good news" to others?
- Evaluate your attitude to those who persecute you. Can you say you have prayed for and forgiven them?

~ 36 ~

DEATH

So you see, just as death came into the world
through a man, now the resurrection from the dead
has begun through another man. Just as everyone dies
because we all belong to Adam, everyone who belongs
to Christ will be given new life. But there is an order to
this resurrection: Christ was raised as the first of the harvest;
then all who belong to Christ will be raised when he comes
back. After that the end will come, when he will turn the
Kingdom over to God the Father, having destroyed every
ruler and authority and power. For Christ must reign
until he humbles all his enemies beneath his feet.
And the last enemy to be destroyed is death.
– 1 CORINTHIANS 15:21-26

Have you ever been in a place where you were reminded of how small you really are? Perhaps you were in the middle of the ocean or flying in a plane looking down on a big city. Maybe you were standing on a mountain peak or seated in a packed stadium with thousands of cheering fans. Sometimes we feel small and insignificant when we are depressed, alone or are about to confront the end of life.

Everyone faces death differently:

- I have known people who seemed to be glad to leave this earth, and others who fought every step of the way.
- Some people want to die alone, while others call their family to be at their bedside.

- Some want to pass away in the hospital, others in the comfort of their home.
- Some bravely face pain, while others want to numb the anguish as much as possible.
- Some seem to "beat" death, while others merely "give up."

As a minister, I am often asked familiar and important questions concerning death. Here's a short list: "Why does God allow this to happen?" "Where do people go when they die?" and "Does God still heal people?" These are all excellent questions, but let me introduce a fourth: "Where is the character of Christ in death?"

THE CHARACTER OF CHRIST IN DEATH

Death is the result of sin.

Paul writes that the wages of sin is death (Romans 6:23). Iniquity was injected into the nature of every human being after Adam. He was created with the ability to choose and he chose his own way—the opposite direction from God. This is the short answer. It's not eloquent or not necessarily philosophical, but it does make one thing clear: death is cruel and is no respecter of persons. It visits us through many channels. Dying can come by illness, an accident, old age, murder, and many unknown causes. It visits unborn children as well as adults in the prime of life. It can arrive without warning.

Sometimes disobedience can lead to the shortening of one's life. Paul explains: *"Don't be misled—you cannot mock the justice of God. You will always harvest what you plant. Those who live only to satisfy their own sinful nature will harvest decay and death from that sinful nature. But those who live to please the Spirit will harvest everlasting life from the Spirit"* (Galatians 6:7-8).

The apostle's teaching makes sense in most situations but it does not address the death of a child or an innocent bystander being gunned down by a maniac. However, once death was set free, it ran wild.

After death, a person's soul enters eternity.

Some enjoy the presence of Christ and await their eternal rewards. Others are absent from the Lord and await their final judgment. Children of God enter into eternity awaiting the resurrection and the glorified bodies promised to us by Jesus. These bodies are difficult to describe because they will be radically changed from anything we have previously known. They will be free from weakness, sickness, unhealthy thoughts and appetites, and decay. Paul explains. *"Our earthly bodies are planted in the ground when we die, but they will be raised to live forever. Our bodies are buried in brokenness, but they will be raised in glory. They are buried in weakness, but they will be raised in strength. They are buried as natural human bodies, but they will be raised as spiritual bodies. For just as there are natural bodies, there are also spiritual bodies"* (1 Corinthians 15:42-44).

The Bible never teaches that the dead become angels. We are born into humanity and will remain this way for all eternity. Since we were all designed to live forever, it is safe to assume that Christ is preparing a place which will continue to give our existence great meaning, fellowship and productivity. Jesus said, *"Don't let your hearts be troubled. Trust in God, and trust also in me. There is more than enough room in my Father's home. If this were not so, would I have told you that I am going to prepare a place for you? When everything is ready, I will come and get you, so that you will always be with me where I am. And you know the way to where I am going"* (John 14:1-4).

As a child of God, the best is yet to come!

God heals.

Some believe God does not perform miracles anymore. This is rather humorous to me because every day is a miracle—something we cannot explain. For example, we are all familiar with the law of gravity and we know that scientists have been discovering previously unknown stars. We can even explain the earth's rotation and the orbiting of the planets, yet we know nothing when it comes to keeping all of the elements in the galaxy from colliding and destroying the universe. We are observers, but not creators or sustainers. Yes, every day is an amazing miracle, and without God we have no hope.

There is nothing wrong with wanting the Lord to heal our sickness, especially if our motive is to honor Him in all we do. But there should also be a growing desire to be with Christ. Paul's perspective on life and death should become ours as well. He writes, *"For to me, living means living for Christ, and dying is even better"* (Philippians 1:21).

Sometimes when we pray for healing we see God intervene; other times He is looking for us to submit so that the final enemy is defeated by the power of Christ. Ultimately, every believer is healed by God, which is the most important truth to embrace and anticipate.

PUTTING IT INTO PRACTICE

Plan your death. Not "how" or "when" you will depart this earth, but Who will be honored. If Christ rules your life then He wants to rule your death. I know a dozen or more people who placed their faith in Jesus Christ AFTER the person they loved or admired died. One person said it this way: "I watched him live and I was impressed. I watched him die and was convinced." This is how the character of Christ is seen in death!

Live with your memorial service in mind. How do you wish to be remembered? Almost every such service features positive testimonies about the deceased, but once in a while we experience a funeral that is not bound by time constraints or the typical last respects. People attend because their lives have been irreversibly influenced by the person they came to honor.

POINTS TO PONDER

- Has someone close to you died? If they were Christ-followers, how did it affect you?
- Have you ever been asked: "Why would God allow this to happen?" or "Why do good people die?" How do you respond?
- Describe your funeral. Who will attend? What will they say about you? What would you *like* them to say?

ESSENTIAL NUMBER FOUR

REPRODUCING CHRIST IN OTHERS

Knowing and experiencing the person of Jesus Christ increases our desire to become dedicated followers. And following Him consistently requires living an obedient lifestyle. Then, as a result, it produces His likeness in us.

As Christ's character takes residence and increases in influence, we begin to do what He does—reproduce His life in others. You and I cannot and *will not* become Jesus Christ, now or in eternity. But the life He has given radiates through us so His salvation and likeness can be duplicated in those He allows us to reach.

Everything God created—such as flowers, trees, animals and people—was designed to procreate. And healthy Christians reproduce healthy Christians.

It is very difficult, if not impossible, for a follower of Jesus to claim spiritual maturity without becoming a "reproducer" of Christ in others. Who we are and what we love cannot be hidden or contained; we pass it on.

Here's the good part. Other than salvation, there is no greater joy in the Christian life than to invest in others and witness God's miraculous power at work in the process. To replicate Christ in the life of another is to see that person come to know Him, follow Him, become like Him, and to reproduce His life all over again in someone else.

~ 37 ~
INVITE THEM

Andrew went to find his brother, Simon, and told him,
"We have found the Messiah" (which means "Christ").
Then Andrew brought Simon to meet Jesus.
– JOHN 1:41-42

I was just a boy in elementary school, sitting on the front porch of our home with a new friend of mine. We were eating the lunch mom had prepared. Before we ate, I simply said, "I'll say grace." So I bowed my head and spoke a little prayer, thanking God for the food, ending with the phrase "In Jesus' name, Amen."

Immediately, I brought the sandwich up to my mouth and took a big bite. While I was chewing, my friend was staring at me with an inquisitive expression. After swallowing a mouthful of sandwich —my mom taught me to never talk with food in my mouth—I asked him, "What's the matter?"

To my shock, he said, "Who is God?"

He was referring to the first couple of words in my prayer: "Dear God." In child-like fashion, I responded with surprise: "You don't know who God is?"

As plain as day and without hesitation, he told me that he had no idea who I was talking about. I don't remember my response, but I do recall what happened about five minutes later. Together, we asked Jesus if He would forgive my friend of his sins and come to live in his heart!

This story didn't take place because I was such a good little boy. It occurred because praying over my food was normal behavior in our family. I didn't know anything different. It happened because I was having lunch with a young friend who had never before heard or witnessed a prayer—and because God was there with two buddies having an innocent and truthful conversation. I can't recall his name, and do not know what became of him, but I do understand how the event taught me that people are more ready to hear about God than we are often ready to share.

Reproducing Christ in Others Starts with an Invitation

Invite people who are interested in a relationship.

Loneliness is more common than any of us realize, and an invitation is the doorway to a new friendship. We all influence others for good or bad, or both. An invitation is about introducing people into a relationship with you and Christ—even though the formal introduction may come at a later time. When you welcome others into a friendship, they are also exposed to your environments, including your family, friends and church.

Those who seek fellowship are not hostile toward the idea of God or the people of the Lord. In fact, many who are "on the outside looking in" merely need an invitation. God has brought them into your life for a reason, and now it's your turn.

The Christian world often makes things too complicated. While it is good, desirable and biblical for us to be able to defend our faith, it is not a prerequisite to inviting your friends to join you on Christ's path. For example, the disciple Andrew did not know all the details concerning Christ before inviting his brother, Simon, to meet the Lord. He thought Jesus may be the "One" they were looking for. Here's the point: *it is normal to invite others to experience what we are experiencing.*

When we discover a great restaurant, we tell our neighbors, friends and family. It's the same with locating a good retail store, seeing an outstanding movie or getting excited about where we have traveled. Our enthusiasm motivates and encourages them to follow in our footsteps. More significantly, when we meet outstanding people, we speak highly of them and aren't bashful introducing our friends to others.

The apostle Paul declared, *"For I am not ashamed of this Good News about Christ. It is the power of God at work, saving everyone who believes...This Good News tells us how God makes us right in his sight. This is accomplished from start to finish by faith"* (Romans 1:16-17).

Why *should* Paul be ashamed? The Gospel transformed his life! Although some may not appear interested in your invitation, at least you will leave an obvious and positive impression concerning the impact Christ has had on you personally. Don't be surprised to find out someday how your words moved that person toward God.

Invitations have much to do with good timing.

Generally speaking, people are more open to invitations during times of change—when their emotions are stirred. Those going through either positive or negative experiences are usually ready for new concepts and ideas. For example, when individuals move from one region to another, they usually welcome new relationships. Or, when children begin attending school, parents will sometimes consider their children's spiritual needs. Experiencing difficulties in finances, health and relationships will often cause a search for godly wisdom and wise counsel.

The Lord has a way of using unusual circumstances to draw people to Himself. Solomon reminds us how God has placed an inner realization of our timeless need—an eternal and perfect connection with our Creator— within each person: *"He has also set eternity in the hearts of men"* (Ecclesiastes 3:11 NIV). Being a good "inviter" is about recognizing when God softens the hearts of those around you and taking advantage of the moment.

Invite people in your own style.

Trust in the presence of Christ, but remember He desires to work through your uniqueness, so let Christ live "through" you.

When water flows through our coffee makers, it comes out the other side as a delicious cup of java. The water is still present, but it has been filled and changed by the presence of the ground coffee beans. In the same way, God flows in your life—which makes your influence special and effective.

Do what you do best with what God has given you. Allow Him to use you in His way, and in His time. Whether your gift is hospitality, serving, evangelism, encouragement or intercession—prayerfully offer yourself to God to help those around you.

As you meet new people and fresh opportunities, remember it is your attitude which will be remembered most. Any gift will be well received if it is given in the Spirit of Christ.

Peter and John were brought before the religious leaders because of their ministry in the name of Christ. Notice how their zealous spirit impacted the religious leaders: *"When they saw the courage of Peter and John and realized that they were unschooled, ordinary men, they were astonished and they took note that these men had been with Jesus"* (Acts 4:13 NIV).

The key phrase in this verse is "they took note" these men had been with Christ. That is, they made a lasting impression because they were the *products* of Jesus. In a sense, they were not of this world. Likewise, when you and I extend our hands in the name of Christ, we do so with a love which goes beyond the passion of a humanitarian. We act as ambassadors of Christ.

PUTTING IT INTO PRACTICE

Regularly ask the Lord to open your eyes to the people and opportunities around you. As He gives you new vision, follow His leading and become His representative. Make a list of people already in your life circle who need to know Christ. Begin to pray for openings to share the Gospel message.

POINTS TO PONDER

- How comfortable are you inviting people into relationship?
- In what way do you think God has specially prepared you for inviting others?
- Can you think of someone who invited you into relationship that made a crucial difference in your life?

~ 38 ~
VALUE THEM

*I have come to call not those who think
they are righteous, but those who know they
are sinners and need to repent.*
– LUKE 5:32

It's confession time. A sister in Christ whom I respected asked me if I would visit her nephew. His name was Phil and he was dying of AIDS. He contacted this deadly disease through a homosexual lifestyle.

We should all know by now that not *everyone* who has AIDS is homosexual or promiscuous, but Phil was both of these. God knew it, he knew it, I knew it—and so did everyone who was acquainted with him.

I visited him in a hospice, located in an old brick house in urban Los Angeles. He was in a room full of natural and unfiltered light, lying still in a hospital-type bed. Phil was unable to walk or speak in a voice louder than a whisper. His body was frail, pale, and thin—and his bed had the odor of death.

Phil could barely acknowledge my presence. To make matters worse, I did not know whether he wanted me there or even knew why I came. I wasn't too sure myself!

This was one of those moments when I didn't know quite what to say. Common phrases seemed irrelevant and out of place. I thought, "Should I introduce myself? Why would he care who I was? I can't ask him how he is doing, that's just stupid."

There was no chair, so I went to the next room and brought one in. Then I sat quietly. Ten minutes or so of silence elapsed before I finally sensed some direction. It seemed the Lord was whispering, "Reach out and put your hand on top of his."

Was this my idea, or God's? I wasn't sure, but that's exactly what I did. I stood up and gently put my hand on top of his frail fingers. Phil slowly turned his head, acknowledging my presence without saying a word. A little while later, I left.

REPRODUCING CHRIST INVOLVES INSTILLING VALUE

People must see that you can look past the obvious.

In Scripture, Jesus walks up to a man named Levi (otherwise known as Matthew) and invites him to become one of His followers. Levi was a sinner and a tax-collector, assessing his own people who were under Roman rule. It was common practice for these men to charge more than was due. This is how they made their living.

Scripture records, *"...as Jesus left the town, he saw a tax collector named Levi sitting at his tax collector's booth. 'Follow me and be my disciple,' Jesus said to him. So Levi got up, left everything, and followed him"* (Luke 5:27-28).

I went back to see Phil. He was stronger—and so was I. That day, I asked him if he was ready to die. His lips moved but I could not hear what he was saying. I lowered my head and put my ear just a few inches away from his lips. In a weak, haltering voice, he responded, "I deserve to go to hell, but I hope God will forgive me."

In that short sentence, I knew more about Phil than almost anyone else on earth. He was not ignorant of his sin, nor of God. All I did was value him enough to visit him and to ask the most relevant question of his life. What was obvious was his imminent death. What was less obvious was his dignity before a gracious God.

When people feel valued, they become reachable.

The story of Levi and Jesus continues. Soon after the Lord invites him to become a disciple, Levi feels so valued he throws a party. Naturally, many of the guests are his friends—fellow tax-collectors and sinners. Who else would associate with a man who robbed his own people?

We read, *Later, Levi held a banquet in his home with Jesus as the guest of honor. Many of Levi's fellow tax collectors and other guests also ate with them. But the Pharisees and their teachers of religious law complained bitterly to Jesus' disciples, "Why do you eat and drink with such scum?"* (Luke 5:29-30).

The church grows when followers of Christ act like Jesus by treating unbelievers with honor, dignity and respect. Then, because of this attitude, when sinners come to the Lord they invite *more* sinners.

It's just that simple. If one Christian becomes an "inviter," and a person accepts, more can follow. Just one Christ-like invitation can result in dozens and even thousands entering into a relationship with Christ.

You value people by looking at them through the eyes of Jesus.

We all know there are many dark and evil souls in this world. There are also tenderhearted people—some who know God and some who don't. Many of the most judgmental people (who look down on their fellow man) can also be religious. So when you pray to be used by the Lord to reproduce His life in others, you should avoid seeing people through the lens of religion. Instead view them through the eyes of Christ.

The moment you decide to bring the Lord to others, you will find yourself in His footsteps: *"Jesus answered them, 'Healthy people don't need a doctor—sick people do. I have come to call not those who think they are righteous, but those who know they are sinners and need to repent'"* (Luke 5:31-32).

In my own words, Jesus is saying: "Many sinners understand they are messed up. They don't need people telling them something they already know. They are looking for an individual who can tell them what they *don't* know."

Remember the AIDS victim Phil? He was preparing himself for hell but hoping God was gracious enough to forgive him. The problem was, he needed someone to give him permission to ask for pardon. When I explained there was no sin too great for God's forgiveness, he went into immediate mourning. Suddenly, he relived all the pain he had caused his parents and those who loved him. He grieved over the fact so many had disowned him: members of his own family and fellow sinners who did not want to look at their potential future. He was truly alone.

Then he prayed. It was only three or four sentences, yet the prayer lasted for about five minutes. It took him that long to speak the words. He could have said them to God in his inner voice, but he wanted me to hear and be his witness.

I wasn't present when he passed from this life, but I did hear him speak many times, and in an affectionate way, the name of Jesus.

I had prejudged him. Even though Phil never knew my name, I was privileged to officiate at his memorial service:

- There was no corpse because his bodily fluids were too dangerous.
- There was no casket because there was no body or money.
- There was no chapel because less than ten people came to honor his life.

Phil was a young man who both lived and died tragically. He went as low as a person can go, but not low enough to miss the grace of God.

PUTTING IT INTO PRACTICE

Are there people you know who don't meet up to your standards? Are you as one of the Pharisees, eager to judge others? Or are you like Jesus who invited and valued people?

I challenge you to consider what Christ modeled when He invited a sinner to follow Him. I want you to remember Phil. I am ashamed of my first attitudes and thoughts toward him. Someday, I hope to ask for his forgiveness.

POINTS TO PONDER

- What pre-judgments might you have which could hinder you reaching out to "sinners"?
- What are some of the ways Jesus valued people others had cast away?
- Have you ever felt the sting of judgment? In what way?

~ 39 ~
FEED THEM

And the King will say, "I tell you the truth, when
you did it to one of the least of these my brothers and
sisters, you were doing it to me!"
– MATTHEW 25:40

The American church tries to encourage young people to experience a short-term mission trip to various poverty-stricken places around the world. We prepare them to go and serve, but what is most often accomplished, at least right away, is a renewed sense of humility. Those who have touched and smelled the reality of what deprivation can bring usually begin to ask questions, ranging from, "How can we end poverty?" to "Why was I born in America?"

I can only think of one thing more humbling and mind-altering than disease and world hunger, and that is eternal judgment. The idea of either everlasting life with God or a never-ending existence apart from Him leaves me with serious questions. As a believer saved by grace, what does God expect of me? What is my contribution? What is within my control and what is left up to someone else? What is God's part? Should I fear the final judgment or should I welcome it?

The Scripture above comes from a prophetic parable told by Jesus. The context of the story is the final judgment, which follows a time (still in the future) of great persecution known as the Tribulation.

The message is clear. People who belong to Christ care for others—even more, they act. And their actions are sacrificial. God's true children are concerned for others even in the midst of personal danger. In this parable Jesus makes it very personal. How we treat people who are hurting is how we treat Him.

REPRODUCING CHRIST
INVOLVES MEETING NEEDS

It was about time for Jesus to be arrested and crucified. His discussions with the disciples and His teaching became increasingly intense. While in Jerusalem, the disciples were innocently admiring the massive man-made structures. In doing so, they created an opportunity for the Lord to teach about the end of time.

Jesus said a day was coming when no building would be left standing (Matthew 24:1-2). In other words, history is racing to an end date when Jesus will return. Later, the disciples asked Him what any one of us would have asked, "When will these things happen?"

The Lord answered with a variety of facts regarding the end times. He told them there will be great deception concerning spiritual matters and wars will increase. Both famines and earthquakes will become common. But all these symptoms are just birth pains before believers will experience great persecution. In short, Jesus explained that love will grow cold and only the Father knows the exact hour when Jesus will return.

Most of Jesus' explanations concerning the end of time were provided within the context of prophetic parables or stories that help the listener visualize the main idea. In His last parable that evening (Matthew 15:31-46), Jesus referred to Himself as the Son of Man, the Shepherd, and King:

- As the Son of Man, He is the judge of all mankind (John 5:27).
- As the Shepherd, He separates the sheep from the goats.
- As King, He will speak the final word.

At the end of history, Jesus will separate people, *"...as a shepherd separates the sheep from the goats. He will place the sheep at his right hand and the goats at his left"* Matthew 25:32-33).

His illustration would have immediately connected with the disciples who were familiar with these animals. Goats are generally mischievous, quarrelsome, and by nature interested in pleasing only themselves. If it were possible, goats would take pride in the idea they are smarter than sheep—just like many non-believers compare themselves to "ignorant and weak" Christians.

Before my wife and I were married, I would visit her at her father's small ranch where one of their two goats would constantly look for an opportunity to run up and ram me from behind. All it took was one butt from that animal to remind me you can't trust a goat. After such an event, I never let that animal out of my sight. Sheep, on the other hand, are much easier to lead. They are mild mannered, simple creatures and, for the most part, follow the directions of the shepherd.

Jesus uses two types of animals that can be seen grazing together, yet anyone can tell them apart. In the same way, though people look similar, God can tell which is which without any hesitation.

Jesus is making three main points.

First: In the end, a person's true identity will be revealed.

Using the Lord's analogy, a person is either a sheep who is led by Christ or a goat. He stated, "*My sheep listen to my voice; I know them, and they follow me. I give them eternal life, and they shall never perish; no one can snatch them out of my hand*" (John 10:27-28 NIV).

Second: All people will be separated into one of two eternal destinations.

The Lord painted many excruciating word pictures to warn people of how horrible it will be to live eternally separated from the presence of God. For example, think what hate, jealousy, self-indulgence and greed can become when God no longer holds back the forces of evil. Speaking of goats, the apostle Paul writes about rebellious hearts: "*...they invent ways of doing evil...they are senseless, faithless, heartless, ruthless. Although they know God's righteous decree that those who do such things deserve death, they not only continue to do these very things but also approve of those who practice them*" (Romans 1:30-32 NIV).

According to Scripture, what makes a person a goat is not just what they do, but also what they *don't*.

Third: Caring for people is not the <u>root</u> of a Christ-follower's faith, it is the fruit.

The people of God have holy hands, not because they look any different, but because they minister to the "least of them."

Jesus often used stern words, and this parable of the sheep and the goats is one example of not only His tenderness toward those in need, but also the seriousness of His warning.

PUTTING IT INTO PRACTICE

Take care of God's flock and bring back His lost sheep. Ask yourself these probing questions:

Do my actions indicate isolation from people and their problems, or are my hands holy hands?

How does my prayer life reveal my knowledge of Christian persecution around the world?

Do I invest my time, talent, and treasure in God's Kingdom or in goat-like behavior?

What opportunities do I have to minister to those around me?

POINTS TO PONDER

- Why do you think Jesus used the analogy of the sheep and goats? Can this still be relevant to us today?
- Do you think it is difficult in our culture to have compassion for others? Why or why not?
- Even though we may not be considered "poor" according to the world's standards, what groups of people might be considered "the least of these" in American society?

~ 40 ~
Inspire Them

*The woman left her water jar beside the well
and ran back to the village, telling everyone, "Come
see a man who told me everything I ever did! Could
he possibly be the Messiah?" So the people came
streaming from the village to see him.*
— John 4:28-30

An enormous amount of good can be found in what we call "normal" human behavior. Common courtesy between one person and another is expected. We teach our children to be polite by using words such as "Please" and "Thank You." It is normal to open a door for a lady and for anyone else coming into a building behind you. It is normal to admit when you have made a mistake, to cooperate with others, to do a good job, and to be responsible.

A step above "normal" is *inspirational.* The spiritual idea of inspiration involves divine influence. Webster defines the word divine to mean, "Of God, like God, or from God." Could we be bold enough to claim such possibilities can exist in and through our lives? Can our actions come from God?

When do you find yourself moved and inspired? Is it in the midst of creation? Is it the mountains, the ocean, the sky, the stars, the prairies? Are you uplifted by heartfelt music or movies re-telling stories of courage and love? What about a passionate speech or sermon? Or perhaps a good book? Are you stimulated by a sincere discussion with a friend? By competition?

Whatever uplifts your spirit draws you in and captures your heart. I hope this is what Jesus has done for you—so much so that your life might become a beacon of inspiration to others.

The story in John 4:1-30 reveals not only who Jesus is but also how He inspired one woman toward the grace of God. He is willing to do similar things through you if you are willing to be His vessel.

REPRODUCING CHRIST INCLUDES AN INSPIRING TOUCH

God inspires others through you when you reach out to them.

Expected behavior includes being kind to all those we meet. However, being inspirational requires doing what is inconvenient—going above and beyond the good and seizing opportunities to be like Christ.

The woman at the well was astonished by her encounter with Jesus the Jew. She *"...was surprised, for Jews refuse to have anything to do with Samaritans..."* (v.9).

What amazed her? There were three major gulfs which separated her from Jesus:

First, there was an ethnic divide. The Jews considered the Samaritan people to be like Gentiles. A typical Jew would never drink from the same cup as a Samaritan because he believed such an act would defile him. The ethnic difference was further strained by history. When the Samaritans built a temple on Mount Gerizim, the Jews destroyed it because they believed proper worship could only be conducted in the temple located in Jerusalem.

The second serious gulf was the disagreement over Scripture. The Samaritans believed only in the Books of Moses (the first five books of the Bible) while the Jews also included the writings of the prophets.

And the third gulf was moral. Jesus, the sinless Son of God, was conversing with a woman who had five sexual partners and was not married to her current companion. Jesus bridged all three gulfs (ethnic, religious, moral) to reach out to this woman at the well. His inspirational actions drew her toward God.

God inspires others through you when you empathize with them.

The conversation between Jesus and the Samaritan woman reveals not only the divinity of Christ but also His humanity. Jesus was thirsty and tired from His travels and really needed a drink of water, but He also empathized with the perpetual thirst of people on this earth. With compassion, Jesus said to the woman, *"Anyone who drinks this water will soon become thirsty again. But those who drink the water I give will never be thirsty again. It becomes a fresh, bubbling spring within them, giving them eternal life"* (vv.13-14).

It is difficult to connect with others if you cannot sympathize with their realities. Jesus uses thirst and water as a connecting analogy to her need. This Samaritan's life history was a living example of a perpetual thirst. Though the text does not reveal why she had five husbands plus her current companion, it implies an unquenchable hunger which was not being satisfied by human methods. Jesus acknowledged her sin without condemning her, because He knew her heart. She did not need angry judgment—she needed help.

God inspires others through you when you give them hope.

Jesus lifted the spirits of the woman at the well by providing answers to her problems. And God will inspire people through you when you provide hope instead of condemnation. This woman was trapped by her past and her present, and her thirst had reached a point of desperation. Jesus offered her hope through a Heavenly Father who was greater than human problems and sin.

The Lord described the Father as one who was looking for worshipers. *"But the time is coming—indeed it's here now—when true worshipers will worship the Father in spirit and in truth. The Father is looking for those who will worship him that way"* (v.23).

What are the qualifications God is looking for in true worshipers? According to Jesus, the Father is searching for those who desire to have a relationship with Him. To worship the Father in Spirit is to commune with God relationally. To worship Him in truth is to come under His authority, to trust in His character and to submit to His leading.

Finally, notice who is qualified for such a relationship—*"anyone who will worship him that way."*

This fallen woman was given hope. Being an "unclean" Samaritan would not disqualify her, nor would being a sinner. She did not need to go to Jerusalem, nor jump through contrived religious hoops. All that was required was a willingness to pursue God in relationship and in truth.

PUTTING IT INTO PRACTICE

You are no longer an infant in the Kingdom. Reproducing Christ in others is not about convenience, rather it requires intentional sacrifice. As a follower of Jesus, it is your calling to glorify, magnify, radiate and reproduce the life of Christ which is within you. Starting today, make a commitment to inspire people and point them toward the Heavenly Father. Reach out to them, empathize and release them with the truth of the Gospel. Begin your spiritual family tree and watch how God inspires others through you!

Now is the time!

POINTS TO PONDER

- What makes a normal action become one that is "inspirational"?
- What does it look like to worship "in spirit and truth"?
- What is the difference between being morally pure and being like Christ?

~ 41 ~
Include Them

*One day as Jesus was walking along the shore of the
Sea of Galilee, he saw two brothers—Simon, also called Peter,
and Andrew—throwing a net into the water, for they fished for
a living. Jesus called out to them, "Come, follow me,
and I will show you how to fish for people!"*
– Matthew 4:18-19

You never know who is going to turn out to be a good disciple, friend and leader. Steven was just starting out in high school, but was already in trouble. He was from a broken home, didn't like school, and he smoked dope. Yet, there was something about this young man I liked. As I made friends with him, he began to confide to me his past struggles and current fears. I was impressed with his openness as he bared his soul.

Some time later I realized why I was drawn to him. A couple hundred teenagers were lining up to enter the meeting place for our weekly youth rally at the church. We were going to observe the Lord's Supper and I had prepared the student leadership, which included Steven, to administer the elements.

While the kids were filing in, Steven pulled me aside and told me he felt uncomfortable participating in communion because he was guilty of sinning earlier that day. He didn't stop there. He told me exactly what he did and I saw the shame rise on his face.

I couldn't help it; I smiled. As he looked at me a bit confused, I put my hand on his shoulder and asked him if he would like to confess the sin to His Savior since he was willing to admit it to me. We prayed together and he not only served the elements with joy, he participated with a renewed sense of celebration for the goodness of God in Christ Jesus.

As I write this story, Steven is married to a pastor's daughter. I can't keep track of how many kids he has because it seems I get an email announcing a new birth on the way every other day! Steven not only finished college, he has also earned a Master's degree in Divinity and is currently raising support to serve as a missionary to Africa.

You'll be amazed what God will do when you include others in the ministry of Jesus Christ!

REPRODUCING CHRIST IS ABOUT INCLUDING

Including people in ministry is to teach them to obey and practice the Great Commission (Matthew 28:18-20).

The Great Commission in Jesus' words to Peter and Andrew is focused on fishing for people. The goal is to make disciples, which is the centerpiece of Christ's command.

Many come to faith believing the goal of a Christian is to become as morally pure as possible. Actually, the objective is to become like Christ. A person can live a moral life by many contemporary definitions, yet be nothing like God's Son. To be Christlike is to mirror Him in character and deed. Perhaps James says it best. "*Now someone may argue, 'Some people have faith; others have good deeds.' I say, 'I can't see your faith if you don't have good deeds, but I will show you my faith through my good deeds'*" (James 2:18).

This definition of morality would include a lifestyle which is consistent with the Great Commission—fishing for people and making them disciples. In essence, this is the activity of reproducing Christ in others.

Including people in ministry is to reveal their true vocation.

Many view their vocation as their job and their significance in terms of how much money they make. Biblically speaking, a disciple of Jesus Christ has one general calling: to glorify God in *all* he or she does while making disciples of Jesus Christ. This vocation is not isolated to the clergy. It is the calling of all followers of Jesus. He states, "*I have been given* call authority in heaven and on earth. Therefore, go and make disciples..." (Matthew 28:18-19).

Being a pastor is my job, not my primary calling. I, like you, am called to make disciples of Jesus Christ. This is my true vocation. Even if I were no longer a pastor, this would not change.

As Christians, we are to be representatives of heaven. *"And God has given us this task of reconciling people to him. For God was in Christ, reconciling the world to himself, no longer counting people's sins against them. And he gave us this wonderful message of reconciliation. So we are Christ's ambassadors..."* (2 Corinthians 5:18-20).

All of us put food on the table and a roof over our heads in different ways and with a variety of skills, but our careers must be seen as one of many opportunities to represent God as ambassadors.

Including people in ministry helps them learn more about dependence on God.

As a spiritual mentor, you should not be embarrassed to ask tough questions, such as: "Tell me about a new person in your life you are influencing toward Christ."

You should also be asking them to help in a ministry within your local church. Assigning such responsibilities may seem bold and pushy, but as they follow your lead, they will grow and learn how to become more dependent on Christ.

Some new believers may think the idea of reaching out to serve people sounds romantic. But meeting the needs of humanity often involves discouraging experiences. Some question your motives, others may strike out against you, become co-dependent, and others disappoint you with their lack of faith.

If you have already been working at making disciples, then you know it is not for the faint of heart. Often the difficulties and failed relationships cause you to take an emotional step back (to re-evaluate the complexities) and then two spiritual steps forward in humility and recommitment.

I often have to remind myself that I'd rather have trials in doing good and obeying my Savior than facing trouble from sinful and self-filled living. And it's for this reason I encourage each new believer to meditate, memorize and openly discuss with me the teaching found in James 1:2-4: *"Dear brothers and sisters, when troubles come your way, consider it an opportunity for great joy. For you know that when your faith is tested, your endurance has a chance to grow. So let it grow, for when your endurance is fully developed, you will be perfect and complete, needing nothing"* (James 1:2-4).

PUTTING IT INTO PRACTICE

At this point, you should be encouraging your new disciples to begin sharing their faith. They should be praying with you about the people God has placed in their life and, when led, inviting them to church. They need to be able to describe what God has done and is doing in their life, then look for opportunities to share their story. In addition, volunteering in or through their local church will help them be connected and learn to lean upon the Lord.

POINTS TO PONDER

- What do you consider your primary vocation?
- Can you think of a defining time when someone has included you in ministry? Describe the experience.
- Do you feel God is placing a certain individual on your heart as a possible disciple? Who? What action will you take?

~ 42 ~
SURROUND THEM

One day soon afterward Jesus went up on a mountain to pray, and he prayed to God all night. At daybreak he called together all of his disciples and chose twelve of them to be apostles. Here are their names: Simon (whom he named Peter), Andrew (Peter's brother), James, John, Philip, Bartholomew, Matthew, Thomas, James (son of Alphaeus), Simon (who was called the zealot), Judas (son of James), Judas Iscariot (who later betrayed him).
– LUKE 6:12-16

One of the most helpful books I have found is *The Master Plan of Evangelism*, by Robert Coleman. It is a "must read" for anyone who desires to be an effective developer of people—a disciple-maker.

In Coleman's classic work, he examines the intentional manner in which Jesus conducted His master plan of making disciples. Though there are a variety of principles at work, the most significant for me was the importance of living the Christian lifestyle within the context of a small group of like-minded, mission-oriented followers of Christ.

I first started creating small group environments when I was a youth pastor. I formed one band of young men by making careful selections, choosing those who proved to be FAT (Faithful, Available, Teachable). Then I began practicing the rest of Jesus' principles that were spelled out in Coleman's book. From the beginning, the guys knew my investment in them came with a price.

My planting of concern, money, relationship and time was sincere and genuine, but there was also an expectation. After our season together came to an end, I expected each of these young men to create their own small group and practice the same things they experienced when they were with me. To this day, I have not found a more effective way to make disciples of Christ. It's amazing how vital fellowship and relationship truly are in the process of maturing. Discipleship is not merely passing on information; it is sharing life itself.

REPRODUCING CHRIST INVOLVES HEALTHY SURROUNDINGS

Surround the new believer with a small group of missions-minded Christians.

The best way to learn Christianity is to *do* Christianity. Unfortunately, many small group activities have been reduced in scope to Bible study and fellowship. Yet, the twelve disciples of Jesus also prayed together, served the needs of others and helped God's Son spread the Good News.

It is very likely we are talking about *your* group. So if your band of disciples has lost their way, there is no better time than the present to renew the purposes and activities of your special fellowship. If you are not part of such a group, take the opportunity to start a new one.

Surround the new believer in a small group with a doctrinally sound leader.

Assisting people in spiritual growth is a dynamic process which includes the teaching of foundational truth, practicing what is learned and sharing the experience with others. It is imperative every new believer participate in a learning environment where sound doctrine is taught. They need to have an opportunity to examine their preconceived ideas and previous behaviors in light of their new life in Christ.

When a person begins to digest good theology, they develop healthy thinking and life-skills. For example, when a convert learns to believe and experience the truths found in the first twelve lessons of this book, they grow in their trust for God. Then, as we trust the Lord *for* and *in* the circumstances of our lives, we receive greater endurance, peace, love and strength. As a result of following Christ, people become healthier in mind and spirit, despite the hardships we often encounter.

Surround the new believer in a small group that is associated with a local Bible-believing congregation.

Too many so-called believers have abandoned the local church and transferred their involvement to a self-directed and self-appointed style of independent Christianity. At first blush, their motives and reasons for "doing church" in their own way sound pure and wholesome—even pleasantly simple. However, dozens of red flags begin to wave in my mind as I see a small group of people swim out to a desert island and separate themselves from what many call "organized religion."

There are all kinds of reasons given for this type of behavior. Some complain the local church is all about money, or it operates like a business. Some believe pastors should not be paid a salary. Others say the church should not own real estate, but give all the money collected to the poor. And the list grows longer. How should we respond to these issues?

I'm not going to say that an organized group of believers who are not part of any local church are bad people, or they are "out to lunch." Sometimes a "house church" makes a lot of sense, but I do have some pointed statements and observations for you to consider.

We have local churches which have made financial mistakes and are repeating those errors even today. But I have found that the people who complain over money in the church are often those who:

1. Reject the biblical principles of Christian stewardship.
2. Have not been involved in the stewardship of local church resources.
3. Do not have a history of working together with others.
4. Are extremely naïve in regard to the life-changing. activities and nature of the local church.
5. Have a difficult time dealing with authority.

Is this true of all? Of course not; nonetheless, we must discern truth in all of our thoughts and behaviors.

We also need to consider some of the other concerns of the local church: whether it operates like a business, has paid staff, and is willing to address the needs of the poor. Healthy homes all involve a certain amount of policies and procedures. The local church is the same. It is a family, yet does have certain business items which must be addressed to create an environment of order. Part of this is to decide how much staffing is prudent to the needs of the body and to evaluate how the church can best reach out to the community and beyond.

All of these activities require obedience to Christ and cooperation with one another—and we cannot run from this high calling. It may be a difficult task, but the church of Jesus Christ is called to be seen in the community in all three modes of experience: visually, audibly and physically. The local church is the hope of the world, a constant reminder of God's presence among us.

PUTTING IT INTO PRACTICE

Read the *Master Plan of Evangelism* by Robert Coleman and apply its principles as you continue your calling to reproduce the life of Christ in others.

POINTS TO PONDER

- What do you feel is the biggest challenge in creating a dynamic small group environment?
- It seems clear that God made us to be relational. How did Christ model this during His ministry?
- What are the most crucial reasons we should surround ourselves with a small group of like-minded Christians?

~ 43 ~
CELEBRATE THEM

***When Jesus heard this, he was amazed. Turning
to the crowd that was following him, he said, "I tell
you, I haven't seen faith like this in all Israel!"***
– LUKE 7:9

I grew up playing traditional American sports—baseball, basketball, and football. I also enjoyed high school wrestling. I figured this would also be the path for my son, Jimmy, until a soccer coach at church constantly tried to recruit him. The coach thought his speed and agility would make him a great soccer player. I was not too enthusiastic because of my traditional sports background, but I agreed to let him give it a try.

The first season did not do much to encourage us. We didn't understand the game and frankly my little boy seemed timid. The season came and passed and I thought "that was that." I was wrong. When the next season rolled around, Jimmy wanted to play. After witnessing a year of timidity and disinterest, I did not expect this to happen.

His first game of the second season will stick out in my mind for as long as I live. In between the first and last whistle, Jimmy had scored five goals. He was aggressive and focused. He demonstrated amazing confidence, enjoyment and skill. My shock quickly turned into interest and my interest into celebration.

Games two, three, and four brought similar results. Jimmy was a soccer player! He was good at all the other sports he played, but he excelled at this. So soccer became a significant activity where his confidence, friendships, personality and recreational enjoyment blossomed. As parents, we celebrated this because it encouraged him to grow in other areas of his life.

REPRODUCING CHRIST IN OTHERS REQUIRES CELEBRATION

Celebrate by being loving with your words.

The Apostle Paul made it clear in his letters to Timothy that their relationship was extraordinary. One of the characteristics which made Paul such an outstanding reproducer of his faith was the depth of his affection. Timothy had to know without a shadow of a doubt that he was loved by Paul. Consider his opening words in 1st and 2nd Timothy:

- 1 Timothy 1:2: *"I am writing to Timothy, my true son in the faith."*
- 2 Timothy 1:2: *"I am writing to Timothy, my dear son."*

Both of these phrases describe affection, bond, connection and relationship. It is not possible to make disciples in the manner Christ described without feeling and expressing these emotions.

Celebrate by revealing positive attributes.

Everyone needs encouragement. Some of us are aware of our positive attributes, while others are not as conscious of them.

Once again, notice how Paul reminds Timothy of his qualities: *"I remember your genuine faith, for you share the faith that first filled your grandmother Lois and your mother, Eunice. And I know that same faith continues strong in you. This is why I remind you to fan into flames the spiritual gift God gave you when I laid my hands on you. For God has not given us a spirit of fear and timidity, but of power, love, and self-discipline"* (2 Timothy 1:5-7).

Why would Paul bother writing what Timothy already knew? Because people forget! Paul was probably discerning that Timothy might be growing weary and fearful in his duties as a pastor. It was a turbulent time. Paul was in prison in Rome and godly leadership was hard to find. In many ways, Timothy was it—a significant leader, yet struggling inside.

An experienced coach will remind his players during a difficult period in the game why they are there, what they are good at, and why they can win. This is exactly what Paul did. He reiterated to Timothy that he was from quality stock, *"I know that you sincerely trust the Lord, for you have the faith of your mother, Eunice, and your grandmother, Lois."* In detailing the history of Timothy's faith, he was reminded why he was in a position of leadership.

The apostle also described what Timothy was good at—and why he could triumph: Paul doesn't state the exact gift Timothy possessed because his emphasis was on the *Giver*, more than any particular attribute. Timothy realized his inadequacies, but trusted in the power of Christ within him. Paul reminds Timothy he can win because of what the Spirit gives—a spirit of power, love, and self-discipline.

To be an effective reproducer of Christ in others, you will need to understand the story God is writing in your disciple's life. From time-to-time, you will need to remind this individual what God has done, what He is doing, and what He will do.

There are very few things more powerful than when you, as a trusted mentor, take the time to affirm and articulate the good you see in him or her. When revealing positive attributes is done accurately and sincerely, it fans the flame of God's Spirit in the disciple.

Celebrate immediately.

Jesus was exceptional at giving immediate feedback. Once He ran into a Roman officer who believed He could heal without needing to be physically present. This officer's faith in Jesus was without question and Christ celebrated this. "When Jesus heard this, he was amazed. Turning to the crowd that was following him, he said, "I tell you, I haven't seen faith like this in all Israel!" (Luke 7:9).

Notice the exclamation mark. Jesus does not just make an observation, He shouts it out. The Lord rejoiced in this disciple's belief without reservation.

Each of us who desire to be good mentors will do well to speak affectionately, to build up with positive words of encouragement, and to make a big deal out of even small things which demonstrate spiritual growth. For those of us who want to make more and better disciples of Jesus Christ, we must express God's heart when they reveal positive progress. We are called to teach them how to celebrate the goodness of God!

PUTTING IT INTO PRACTICE

As a spiritual mentor, notice the strengths of those you are developing and rejoice with them. At first, give easy assignments that will build confidence and increase their interest in walking with God. For example, encourage them to memorize the names and order of the books of the Bible or expose them to an opportunity to serve the needy. Give them specific tasks to accomplish and celebrate their obedience!

POINTS TO PONDER

- Why is it so important to continually encourage others in their positive attributes?
- What are some ways you can express to others the positive growth you see in them?
- Can you share a time when someone really encouraged you to "press on"? Describe it.

~ 44 ~
EQUIP THEM

*You have heard me teach things that have
been confirmed by many reliable witnesses. Now
teach these truths to other trustworthy people who
will be able to pass them on to others.*
– 2 TIMOTHY 2:2

Everybody's story is different. Some of us have been raised in a religious environment that lacked spiritual edification and equipping. Many have been brought up in moral surroundings which lacked spiritual awareness. Others come from an extremely dysfunctional environment, and a select few have been raised in a nurturing home filled with emotional, relational and spiritual health.

I was blessed to grow up in a good home. We were not a perfect family, yet we experienced a healthy dose of emotional, relational, and spiritual nutrition. All of the kids were given chores to do. We were expected to do well in school, and had family meetings centered on spiritual themes. We played together, were taught social manners and attended and participated in a local church. Yes, we had our share of disagreements, but we were disciplined, rewarded and treasured. All in all, we were a family that provided a healthy home where growth could happen.

Unfortunately, I did not always appreciate the fertile soil in which I was raised. It was not until I was in my mid-twenties and working in the business world when I finally realized the riches of my spiritual upbringing. Before this time, I had no idea how significantly one's heritage could affect behaviors and values—and didn't fully comprehend how much Christ was needed in society.

REPRODUCING CHRIST REQUIRES EQUIPPING OTHERS

Equipping is about doctrine.

The doctrine of a misdirected life is satisfied feelings and immediate gratification. As humans, we want *what* we want *when* we want it. As transformed followers of Jesus Christ, what we desire is God. Wanting Him is having a relationship with truth. And sound doctrine concerns digesting this truth, regardless of what we initially think. In the long run it is truth that makes us strong and frees us from small thinking and behaviors.

As guides for new believers, we have a responsibility to teach them sound doctrine. At first, this kind of teaching is deductive (we tell them what the Bible teaches). In such instruction, you become the agent of God, and your duty is to be well-grounded in essential doctrines while at the same time admitting you do not know all the answers. As a new believer grows and is able to grasp essential elements of the faith, learning becomes more inductive (truth is discovered as one interacts with God's Word alone or in study groups with other believers).

When we teach young boys and girls about baseball, we start with the fundamentals, telling them how to play the game. As they grow older, they remain true to the timeless principles of the sport, but they also grow, learn and apply themselves in ways which go far beyond what we taught them in the beginning. In a similar way, new believers need to be guided, grow through the life process, and then continue reproducing by guiding others.

Equipping is about development.

To equip a new believer is to teach them what and how to pass on all they have learned. The "what" is always about the essentials of the Gospel, while the "how" concerns making disciples. Paul wrote, *Teach these great truths to trustworthy people who are able to pass them on to others.*

Notice the "how" includes investing your time and teaching to those who prove to be trustworthy.

We understand that all of us fail and make mistakes, but to help form a reproducing disciple requires trust. And when this confidence is broken it must be addressed. To be an effective mentor is much like being a loving parent, even though you are dealing with another adult. You must confront the problem of unfaithfulness because it *begets* unfaithfulness —just as faithfulness produces faithfulness.

Like Timothy, your assignment as a follower of Jesus is to entrust the Great Commission and all you have learned to those who will continue the process until the Lord returns.

The primary question you must ask is, "Are they developing?" If they are, no matter how slowly, continue on. If you cannot see progress in their faith and obedience with the truth you have presented—and what God is using to test them— then you must take the next step.

Equipping is about discipline.

Time and time again, you will see more people fall away from the faith than you will see grow in the Lord. This is sad and unfortunate, yet it is the truth (see the Parable of the Soils, Luke 8:4-21). When your effort to equip another believer is not being received, you must speak the truth. It's not pleasant, but when done with a pure heart, it is just as loving as giving someone a hug— even though it may not feel like it!

It appears Timothy might have been tempted to waiver in the face of hardship, so Paul addresses the issue: *"Endure suffering along with me, as a good soldier of Christ Jesus. And as Christ's soldier, do not let yourself become tied up in the affairs of this life, for then you cannot satisfy the one who has enlisted you in his army. Follow the Lord's rules for doing his work, just as an athlete either follows the rules or is disqualified and wins no prize.*

Discipline is consistently doing the right things even in the face of discouraging elements. It is about giving when the finances are tight, serving when no one seems to appreciate your effort, doing what is right when everyone else seems to be doing what is easy. If you don't model and teach discipline, you will fail in your quest to make more and better disciples of Jesus Christ.

PUTTING IT INTO PRACTICE

Make it clear to your disciples what you expect them to do and be. Describe and model for them what you are looking for and what the Lord expects.

POINTS TO PONDER

- According to 2 Timothy 2:1-5, what traits should we be looking for in a disciple?
- In being an "agent of God," what are our responsibilities?
- How would you define discipline in the context of mentoring a disciple?

~ 45 ~
CHALLENGE THEM

*One day Jesus called together his twelve
disciples and gave them power and authority
to cast out all demons and to heal all diseases. Then
he sent them out to tell everyone about the Kingdom
of God and to heal the sick. "Take nothing for your journey,"
he instructed them. "Don't take a walking stick, a traveler's bag,
food, money, or even a change of clothes. Wherever you go,
stay in the same house until you leave town. And if a town
refuses to welcome you, shake its dust from your feet as
you leave to show that you have abandoned those people
to their fate." So they began their circuit of the villages,
preaching the Good News and healing the sick.*
– LUKE 9:1-6

Brett grew up in my youth group. I liked him; he was one of my favorites. He had a good heart and was always cooperative. While attending Biola University, he became a youth ministry intern at a church in California where I was the pastor. I hoped he would serve full-time on my staff in the future. My wish was realized a few years later, but in a different church and in another state.

As expected, Brett was doing a fine job, but I began to notice some things that didn't seem quite right. I knew him well and it didn't appear he was having much fun, and his sense of humor was not as healthy as in years past. I approached him concerning this and we began a discovery process to see if what I was sensing had any validity. I trusted his ability to think over the conversation and at a later time to reveal his honest thoughts.

We unearthed several things that changed the course of his ministry. His expectations for youth work did not match the vision within the church and the demands of the young people seemed to impede Brett's desire to learn and to educate. Brett loves to read, study and pass this knowledge on to enthusiastic students; he enjoys reason and philosophy, challenging and equipping the way people think.

It was hard to see Brett leave. I loved playing basketball with him. I really enjoyed his family. I was proud of him when he would speak at our Sunday services. But now I am even prouder at how the Lord is using him. Today, he travels across the country to talk to parents and students. He is furthering his education and continues to have opportunities to speak on the radio and at public events. Brett is in his element and more is yet to come!

Reproducing Christ Calls For an Occasional Challenge

Challenge your disciple by trusting him with more responsibility.

That's what God's Son did when He called the twelve together and gave them power and authority to cast out demons and to heal all diseases. *"Then he sent them out to tell everyone about the coming of the Kingdom of God..."* (Luke 9:2).

You may not be able to bestow your disciple the power Jesus had, yet you have more influence than you might think. Helping a person discover strengths and spiritual gifts is one of the first steps. Giving them permission to apply their talents and skills is where growth begins.

I saw something solid in Brett from the time he was a young teenager. He was willing to learn and exuded a humble spirit. I suggested that he had an influencing presence and encouraged him to use it for God's purposes inside and outside of the church. And I constantly gave him more responsibilities in ministry and challenged him in his relationships at school and at home. He didn't disappoint me. This is not to say he never made a mistake, but he always met difficult situations with an open mind and a willing heart.

Challenge your disciple to step out of his or her comfort zone to serve.

As the twelve prepared for their adventure with Jesus, He told them not to take anything along on their journey: *"Don't take a walking stick, a traveler's bag, food, money, or even a change of clothes"* (Luke 9:3).

By doing this, Jesus was teaching His disciples to minister from a position of faith in God rather than one of self-sufficiency. It's human to do what is easy, but growth happens when we step outside our comfort zone and serve beyond our experience.

I think back to Brett in his early years. He was comfortable being a loyal follower, doing just about everything a leader could expect. He attended, invited friends, came prepared and he was willing to be vulnerable in discussions. So, in front of his colleagues, I asked him to stretch and grow—to learn how to express what God meant to him and what he thought the Lord might be teaching. I think he knew that I wouldn't take "no" for an answer.

His public speaking debut was well received. So well, in fact, he began regularly teaching his peers. After a while, Brett became a known and respected leader within his circles of influence. Almost naturally, he became an intern youth director and was making a difference.

Challenge your disciple by preparing him for opposition, just as Jesus did.

The Lord explained what was possible and He prepared them with appropriate instructions, including what to do if a town refused to welcome them. In such cases, the disciples were told to *"...shake its dust from your feet as you leave to show that you have abandoned those people to their fate"* (Luke 9:5).

Opposition is a normal part of leadership, being a Christian and trying to live a godly life. And it is most certainly an expected part of being a disciple-maker!

In our small group, we would often discuss the resistance godly leaders might face in various circumstances. At school and work it is usually in the form of rejection and ridicule. At church and home, hostility is often expressed in some form of jealousy and unfair judgment. This can include a lack of affirmation and cooperation.

Discussing the realities of opposition is helpful, but it is not enough: Disciples need to know more than the facts:

- They need to understand how to stand alone.
- They need to know how to love people in spite of how they behave.
- They need to learn why people act as they do.
- They need to learn how to look deeper than the surface behaviors of those who oppose them.
- They need to know when to persevere and when to move on to other opportunities.

Because there are no easy answers, a mentor must remain connected to their disciple as they move "beyond comfortable" to serve others.

PUTTING IT INTO PRACTICE

As the relationship between a mentor and a disciple matures, it is normal for them to meet less often. After all, each person should be making more and better disciples of Jesus Christ. But it is still healthy to stay in touch to maintain a sense of relational and spiritual support.

POINTS TO PONDER

- Can you remember a time God called you out of a "comfort zone" to serve?
- How can giving someone more responsibility challenge them?
- What advice did Jesus give us in Luke 9:1-6 regarding facing opposition? How can we apply His advice today?

~ 46 ~
SUPPORT THEM

"Simon, Simon, Satan has asked to sift each of you like wheat. But I have pleaded in prayer for you, Simon, that your faith should not fail. So when you have repented and turned to me again, strengthen your brothers."
– LUKE 22:31-32

Above the door in my office, written in large letters is the word "FINISH." It's there because the urge to do something easier comes around more often than I like to admit. There are many distractions for all God's people, and for servant-leaders, there is often a temptation to quit.

Giving up starts on the inside and the reasons for such action are numerous. At certain times we feel we are not making a positive contribution. We may be faced with opposition, or have grown weary because we have not taken good care of our body, emotions, mind and heart. Sometimes we have undisclosed sin in our closet waiting to walk out in the light and expose us for who we really are. Or, we forget why we were called to leadership in the first place.

As the temptation to quit increases, it causes leaders to lose perspective. They begin to see everything that is wrong instead of looking at all the good the Lord is doing. Seeds of negativity germinate—and they begin blaming others, or they embark on a personal pity party. Suddenly, the leader begins to gaze over the fence to see if the grass is greener elsewhere.

Many vistas look inviting from a distance, yet the closer you get, the more things stay the same. If leaders walk alone, they will drift from the mission and may abandon their post—not being able to enjoy the fruit of their faithfulness. The artificial turf will draw them away and they will fail without help or encouragement.

REPRODUCING CHRIST INVOLVES PERSONAL SUPPORT

Support your disciples by helping them see potential problems.

Jesus warned Peter with this startling statement: *"Simon, Simon, Satan has asked to sift each of you like wheat"* (Luke 22:31).

Are Christ's words true for every believer, or only for Peter? According to Scripture, Satan's desire is ruin anyone he can. Years later, Peter wrote. *"Stay alert! Watch out for your great enemy, the devil. He prowls around like a roaring lion, looking for someone to devour"* (1 Peter 5:8).

How does the enemy attack you and your disciple? Any way possible! But the most common method is to work in the secret areas of our lives, often called the dark side of our souls.

Usually, our well-known weaknesses don't knock us down because those who love us confront and hold us accountable for our actions. The most dangerous failings, and the ones the devil will try to exploit, are those we attempt to keep hidden.

We conceal our sins for many reasons. Sometimes it's because we want to believe we will conquer them before they are exposed. Or, we hide our wrongs because we know it may mean we will have to step down from a leadership role. It could be we are ashamed and imagine great humiliation will result if we let our weaknesses out into the light of day. Sometimes we cloak our sin in secrecy because we actually *like* it—and don't want to let it go.

Bringing our trespasses out in the open will take away much of their power, but we usually need a persistent and trusting friend or mentor to accomplish this. There are no guarantees, but there are a few things you can do.

First, remember that healthy relationships take time to form. If you share some of your frailties and past sins, it will invite those you are with to do the same.

Second, read books with your disciple which help enlighten and explain some of the reasons why we do stupid things. Engage them in a discussion about their reading. As they test the waters of honesty with you, realize that they will be watching your reactions carefully to see if you will reject, ridicule or blame them.

Finally, be guarded how you talk about other people and their problems. If you repeat confidential information about others, it is easy for a person to believe you will do the same to them.

Support your disciple by praying for them.

After warning Simon Peter about the devil's intent, Jesus provides personal support. He says, *"But I have pleaded in prayer for you, Simon, that your faith should not fail"* (Luke 22:32).

Notice Jesus' strategy. He does not overwhelm Himself by adopting a thousand disciples; He chooses twelve and invests Himself in them. If you focus on a small group of people, your prayer life will become more concentrated. You will not be overburdened with the plight of the world, but with the needs of those the Lord has placed in your circle of influence.

During prayer times, bring your disciple regularly before the Lord, and don't hesitate to pray for them while they are in your presence. Let them know you continually bring them before the Father. This is what Jesus did, because prayer changes things—and it reminds the person their life counts and they are loved.

Support your disciple by being realistic.

Realism provides a sense of acceptance. Jesus says, *"So when you have repented and turned to me again, strengthen your brothers"* (Luke 22:32). Don't be afraid to tell those you are investing in that they may stumble. It's not a matter of "if," but "when." You should not mention this as a prospect you are looking forward to, or because you have low expectations, rather it is a reality.

On occasion God allows us to fail and reap the consequences so we might grow in our understanding of how devastating even "smaller" sins can be. These kinds of experiences have a potentially positive outcome. We listen better, lean more upon the Lord, recognize our weaknesses, pray more often and celebrate God's grace.

If we don't speak truth concerning failure we create an unrealistic relationship which is headed for great disappointment. In fact, expectation not based on reality is one of the primary causes of relational fractures. While we strive to be holy, we do so because God is holy and we desire to please Him. It is not so we might become accepted—because we already are.

PUTTING IT INTO PRACTICE

Encourage your disciple to expand his or her knowledge of self. There are many books which do an excellent job describing personality, spiritual gifts, strengths and weaknesses.

In recent years, much progress has been made in the understanding of how our dark sides have both positive and negative potential. Books on leadership which include overcoming human frailties will also prove invaluable to discovering what makes us tick.

POINTS TO PONDER

- What are some of the primary reasons leaders are tempted to quit?
- Name a few tangible ways we can show our support to a disciple?
- How can we help those we mentor get to know themselves better? How may this contribute to his or her success?

~ 47 ~
Confront Them

Peter said, "Lord, I am ready to go to prison with you, and even to die with you." But Jesus said, "Peter, let me tell you something. Before the rooster crows tomorrow morning, you will deny three times that you even know me."
– Luke 22:33-34

He was outgoing, knew all the right things to say, and seemed spiritually well-qualified to be an elder in the church. I asked him if he would like to be a candidate to serve in this capacity and he readily accepted. Next, I submitted his name to the church body expecting full support. But that's not what happened.

I received a very humble and concerned call from one of the couples in our church regarding this particular candidate for eldership. I was surprised, but knew these people well and made an appointment to listen to their concerns. While sitting in their living room, I could tell they felt quite uncomfortable yet compelled to share certain information with me. I could sense their love for the Lord, the church, and doing the right thing— no matter how hard it might be. They talked; I listened.

After clarifying a few issues, I was convinced I needed to confront the candidate. So I made an appointment and told him ahead of time what it was about. He came into my office and we discussed the matters which had been brought to my attention. It was awkward, but it ended with him withdrawing his name as a candidate.

If you enjoy confronting people regarding their mistakes, weaknesses and character flaws, something must be wrong with you! Unfortunately, most of us have met people who seem to enjoy pointing out the imperfections they see in others. Jesus calls this kind of person a hypocrite: *"Why do you look at the speck of sawdust in your brother's eye and pay no attention to the plank in your own eye? How can you say to your brother, 'Let me take the speck out of your eye,' when all the time there is a plank in your own eye? You hypocrite, first take the plank out of your own eye, and then you will see clearly to remove the speck from your brother's eye"* (Matthew 7:3-5 NIV).

As Christians, we have a responsibility to warn and correct each other. Frankly, I do not relish this aspect of ministry, but it is required to participate in the reproducing of Christ's life in others.

REPRODUCING CHRIST INCLUDES CONFRONTATION

Confront your disciple on a regular basis.

It's like an earthquake theory I once heard while living in California. I was told that the more small quakes we felt, the safer we were from a devastating quake that would result in hundreds or thousands losing their lives. The logic has to do with the build-up of tension at the fault lines. If the tension is relieved, the less likely it is for a major shift to occur.

I'm not sure if this is scientifically valid, but I do believe this is true in relationships, especially when you're trying to assist others in spiritual growth.

When we ignore potential problems, tension mounts. And if we hold things inside instead of facing them, we are building toward a major blow-up.

The problem with confrontations is that many of them are unnecessary, but honest and healthy discussion can eliminate the potential for a virtual detonation. Explosions are often so emotional that little benefit can come from them. Much is said and exaggerated, resulting in hurt feelings and regrets.

When we calmly discuss disagreements as a normal part of a relationship, we learn that a small dose of regular conflict is actually healthy. This style of relating teaches how opposing opinions can exist without threatening the overall goal and satisfaction of both parties. It also teaches that conflict is the door to relational acceptance and intimacy.

The goal of mentoring a disciple is not to develop a person who looks, thinks, and acts exactly like the mentor. Though some of this will naturally occur, the objective has more to do with discovering, equipping and celebrating what God has done and will do in and through this unique person who is committed to Jesus Christ.

Confront your disciple when it really matters.

Facing contention does not mean we need to comment on everything a new believer does wrong or not to perfection. It isn't about nagging, and certainly not about legalism. Rather, confrontation is concerned with developing convictions and values which reflect the image of Christ. These are discovered within the four essentials of Christian maturity—knowing Christ, following Him, becoming like Him, and reproducing Him.

These identify the dimensions of cooperation *with* God which produce trust *for* God, devotion *to* God, character *like* God, and a mission-minded lifestyle in line with the great commission and the great commandment.

When we confront, our primary focus should not be on the surface behavior, rather on the root of the problem.

Jesus told Peter he was going to deny Him three times before the crow of the rooster. He said this after He faced Peter on an underlying issue, which was his faith. Peter did not think this was a problem, so he responded to Jesus with these words, *"Lord, I am ready to go to prison with you, and even to die with you"* (Luke 22:33).

Only then did Christ bring up the behavior, because He knew Peter's issue was trust. Wise mentors focus on root causes, misguided values and spiritual convictions.

Confront your disciple with deep affection.

When we confront out of frustration and anger, the message we send rarely connects—and if it does, it usually communicates what we don't want to say.

"You have made me mad and I'm sick of your behavior." This type of showdown teaches your disciple to run and hide. It is not transformational and does not produce change.

An exchange born out of frustration is not incarnational. That is, it doesn't represent Christ alive in you. Too much of *you* will bring out too much of *them,* and both of you will miss out on the presence of the Spirit working in and through a relationship of godly affection.

The test of an elder is love and patience, not knowledge. A carnal man has the capacity to attain a great wealth of information and still not be transformed.

In biblical terms, the knowledge of God is as much or more concerning a walk with the Almighty as it is the articulation of good doctrine and theology. So the test of a mentor is closely associated with the requirements of an elder. Notice how Paul describes how both of these must conduct themselves: *"Teach the older men to exercise self-control, to be worthy of respect, and to live wisely. They must have strong faith and be filled with love and patience"* (Titus 2:2).

PUTTING IT INTO PRACTICE

As mentors and disciple-makers who are reproducing the life of Christ in others, your greatest challenge is to be the type of person described in Titus 2:2. Please memorize this passage and consider making it one of your life verses.

POINTS TO PONDER

- How can confrontation actually be beneficial in relationship?
- What qualities are essential to maintain when a serious encounter is necessary?
- What will the consequences be if we avoid needed confrontation?

~ 48 ~
FORGIVE THEM

After breakfast Jesus asked Simon Peter,
"Simon son of John, do you love me more than
these?" "Yes, Lord," Peter replied, "you know I love
you." "Then feed my lambs," Jesus told him. Jesus repeated
the question: "Simon son of John, do you love me?" "Yes,
Lord," Peter said, "you know I love you." "Then take care
of my sheep," Jesus said. A third time he asked him,
"Simon son of John, do you love me?" Peter was hurt
that Jesus asked the question a third time. He said,
"Lord, you know everything. You know that I love
you." Jesus said, "Then feed my sheep.
– JOHN 21:15-18

W hen I was a youth minister, my pastor trusted me with the oversight of the church while he went on a much deserved extended vacation with his family. I was eager to do a good job with my additional duties. My assignment was to teach at each service every weekend, administer several baptisms, oversee a building project and handle other day-to-day responsibilities of a senior pastor.

Most things ran smoothly, but one situation was impossible to ignore. After Sunday morning services concluded, I turned the water on to fill the baptistery to be used that evening. I knew this would take several hours, giving me plenty of time to enjoy lunch out with family and friends. Unfortunately, I was having such a good time, I completely forgot about the water running!

About an hour before the evening service was to begin, I drove up to the church property and saw a small stream of water trickling from the overflow baptistery pipe. My heart sank! Immediately, I remembered what I had done. So I parked the car and began running toward the problem. But I was too late.

Not knowing I was responsible, Mike, a hard-working deacon, came around the corner to greet me and said in a panic, "The whole worship center is flooded!"

We both entered the building and I could not believe my eyes. "Flooded" was the correct word for the day! I could have also added words such as embarrassed, ashamed, stupid, careless, rookie—you get the idea!

After telling Mike what had happened, we both did our best to squeegee out as much water as possible before the evening services began. We tried to make light of the situation by speaking of Noah and the great flood, but we all knew the damage was done.

When the pastor returned from vacation, I did what a lot of kids do when they get in trouble. I carefully related all the wonderful things that happened while he was gone—how we truly missed him and were glad he was back. I reported the progress of the construction project, attendance figures, and anything else that sounded good before I walked him into the worship center to see the aftermath of the flood.

After shaking off the initial shock, he was his true self. Instant forgiveness was in the air and his problem-solving skills went right to work. Six months later, with the help of a new vision for the worship center, insurance funds and generous donations, we enjoyed a completely remodeled place to worship together.

REPRODUCING CHRIST WILL NOT HAPPEN WITHOUT FORGIVENESS

Forgive your disciple because you love God.

As a mentor and a maturing believer, love is your greatest attribute. It is probably easier to empathize and forgive a person who floods a worship center accidentally than it is to pardon moral failure or personal betrayal. Nonetheless, if we are to excel at anything, it should be forgiveness.

Knowledge of the Almighty and fellowship with His Spirit cultivates faith, hope and love. Yet, we know from the famous 13th chapter of 1 Corinthians that love is the greatest of these.

Loving God is about honoring and obeying Him from the depth of our heart. Jesus tells us, *"Just as I have loved you, you should love each other"* (John 14:32).

Forgiveness fits perfectly into this picture. When we adopt a person as our spiritual son or daughter (as Paul described his relationship with Timothy) forgiving them is consistent with this type of dedication. It is how we demonstrate and make visible the love we have for God. Said in another way, when we love the Lord, people receive forgiveness and His presence is seen in us.

Forgive your disciple because you love people.

We must view our fellow man through the eyes of Christ—which causes us to truly love them. It's almost as if we can go back to the very beginning and see God's intent as He created all things. We can feel the intensity of His love and great disappointment due to Adam's fall—and eavesdrop on the conversation of redemption within the community of God—Father, Son, and Spirit. We are able to rise above the obvious heartbreak of humanity and see God's ultimate plan of salvation.

From this vantage point, we love people because we can see the fingerprint of the Creator upon them. We recognize they are made in the image of our Lord—and realize we play a part in God's plan of redemption by loving them, even in the midst of their failure and sin. Sure, we are human and mourn the sinful state, but we do not set up permanent residence there. We move through sin by redeeming it with forgiveness.

As Paul explains, *"You must make allowance for each other's faults and forgive the person who offends you. Remember, the Lord forgave you, so you must forgive others. And the most important piece of clothing you must wear is love"* (Colossians 3:13-14).

True love is to forgive.

Forgive your disciple with evidence.

Perhaps you've heard it said, "I forgive you, but I cannot trust you."

One of my teachers made this statement: "Forgiveness is one thing, and trust is something else."

I can't completely disagree with either of these remarks, but I believe Christ would qualify and challenge them.

Obviously we lose trust in people who let us down. This is a normal reaction. We also believe trusting someone who has failed us is not wise. But if we ignore these statements we have become shallow in our faith and will possibly miss great opportunities for redemption.

To forgive is to release from a debt. If we say "I forgive you but I cannot trust as I once did" we are still holding a person's debt against them.

We are naïve to think people don't make mistakes. It's like saying in the beginning of a relationship, "I can trust you since I haven't seen your faults. But once you reveal them, I won't be able to trust you again."

There is another issue: releasing a person from an obligation caused by failure and perhaps sin. This is an intentional decision on your part. To say, "I forgive you" allows the offender to rebuild his or her trust. It's not about you, rather about the person who has failed.

We must never leave someone in the valley of failure with this double-edged sword: "I forgive you, but we can no longer be friends." This is not forgiveness; it is rejection.

Pay careful attention to how Jesus handled Peter when he denied Him, which was a personal betrayal. The Lord pursued Peter, confronted him and tested Peter's regret and desire for reconciliation. Again Jesus asked him, *"'Simon son of John, do you love me?' Peter was hurt that Jesus asked the question a third time. He said, 'Lord, you know everything. You know that I love you.' Jesus said, 'Then feed my sheep'"* (John 21:17-18).

The Lord mended their relationship and cast a vision of the future. It was a framework to rebuild trust and to activate the engine of forgiveness and redemption.

PUTTING IT INTO PRACTICE

When your disciple offends you, it is your opportunity to confront, test, forgive and redirect. Your proactive and redemptive attitude gives opportunity for this person to show his or her true colors. Don't be shocked if failure occurs. Be prepared for it, and remember it's not about you. I believe your disciple will respond positively to your Christlike response.

POINTS TO PONDER

- What are the most compelling reasons the Lord gives us for forgiving others?
- What message can we model by offering pardon?
- What evidence is necessary to show true forgiveness?

NOTES

_____

_____

_____

_____

_____

_____

_____

_____

_____

_____

_____

_____

_____

_____

_____

_____

_____

_____

_____

_____

_____

_____

FOR A COMPLETE LIST OF MEDIA
RESOURCES OR TO SCHEDULE THE AUTHOR FOR
SPEAKING ENGAGEMENTS, CONTACT:

JIM PIPER
CREEKSIDE CHRUCH

PHONE: 303-766-4333
INTERNET: www.creeksidechurch.org